UNDERSTANDING THE

UNDERSTANDING THE

New Birth

DR. JOHN E. WILSON

Understanding the New Birth

St. John's Full Gospel Deliverance Church
27 Brown Street
Bloomfield, CT 06002
Phone: (860) 242-2627
Fax: (860) 726-9648
Web site: www.sjfg.org
e-mail: info@sjfg.org

ISBN 0-924748-42-7
UPC 88571300012 3

Printed in the United States of America
© 2004 by John E. Wilson

Milestones International Publishers
4410 University Dr., Ste. 113
Huntsville, AL 35816
(256) 536-9402, ext. 234; Fax: (256) 536-4530
www.milestonesinternationalpublishers.com

Cover by: Tony Laidig - www.thirstydirt.com

1 2 3 4 5 6 7 8 9 10 11 / 09 08 07 06 05 04

DEDICATION

This book is dedicated to my father and mother, Johnny and Lillie Mae Wilson, who were, because of their resolve to walk upright, always a steadying influence and strength for me all of my life.

To my uncle, Bishop J.J. Martin, for his love, mentoring, and guidance for many years. He helped instill in me the foundation and principles of holiness.

ACKNOWLEDGMENTS

This book could not have been written without the time, suggestions, guidance, and support from numerous people. I would like to express to them my most sincere appreciation.

To the entire church family of St. John's Full Gospel Deliverance church in Bloomfield, Connecticut, you always supported me in all of my work. I thank God for you.

Special thanks to Pastor Aaron D. Lewis for sharing his expertise with me and for encouraging me from start to finish.

Thanks to my sons Michael Anthony and Michael Joseph for their continuous love and support.

To my friends and colleagues in the ministry, who have helped in my work for the upbuilding of God's Kingdom. Your wisdom and valuable insight were helpful in this project.

Thanks to Bishop W.E. Fuller, who ordained me and inspired me as a young man to go forth and declare the Gospel of Jesus Christ.

Thanks to my brother, Bishop Harold Benjamin, who has always been a positive influence in my life.

I will forever be grateful for the love and peace of God, who has given me a passion to reach the lost at any cost.

It's an honor and a privilege for me to recommend Dr. John Wilson's *Understanding the New Birth*. Dr. Wilson's exceptional leadership, godly counsel, and articulate wisdom have been an asset to the body of Christ and to me through many years. First Corinthians 4:15 (KJV) reads, *"For though ye have ten thousand instructors in Christ, yet have ye not many fathers...."* Dr. Wilson is one of those rare, true spiritual fathers to many sons and daughters in the Kingdom of God. I personally know that he has a heart for souls and "true salvation."

> *Pastor/Prophetess Sandra Moore*
> *Prophetic Revival Center*
> *Sandra Moore Ministries, Inc.*
> *Homestead, Florida*

Over the past few years, I have had the distinct honor and privilege of getting to know Apostle Wilson both in person and, even greater, by the Holy Spirit. Of all the many apostles and twenty-first-century church leaders, I believe his impeccable reputation and commitment to quality ministry places him among the choicest of God's servants. Our relationship has been the inspiration for the many things that I am now doing in ministry today. I am fully convinced that *Understanding the New Birth* will be a tremendous blessing to all who read it. It will be of far greater benefit to those who choose to read it more than once. My prayer is that Apostle Wilson will continue to write many more books as God has given him much to say in this hour of renewal and refreshing for the body of Christ.

Apostle Nathan Anderson
Greater Myers Chapel Pentecostal
Fellowship Ministries
Charlotte, North Carolina

Over the past forty years, Dr. John Wilson and I have shared many wonderful experiences in the service of the Lord. I can remember a number of occasions where broken, confused, hopeless, exhausted, weary souls were lifted, changed, and set free by the life-changing words that flowed from his lips. I am certain that this book will serve as a midwife in life's delivery room for numerous men, women, boys, and girls who are ready to embrace the experience of the new birth.

Dr. Ardell E. Tucker
Mt. Calvary Deliverance Tabernacle
New Haven, Connecticut

In the more than thirty-two years that I've known Apostle John E. Wilson, I have come to appreciate the consistency of his spiritual character, and I've learned to admire his powerful focus on completing an arduous task. Over the past three decades, I've noticed that Apostle Wilson's passion for winning the lost has not diminished, but rather has accelerated in pace. *Understanding the New Birth* is a written testament of his great passion to win the lost at any cost and then to make disciples of them. This book is a valuable resource to every Bible study group and Sunday school class that is learning the basics of the Christian faith.

Bishop LeRoy Bailey Jr.
Senior Pastor, The First Cathedral
Presiding Prelate, Churches Covered and
Connected in Covenant
Author of A Solid Foundation:
Building Your Life from the Ground Up

Apostle J.E. Wilson is one of the patriarchs of the deliverance movement in America. In addition, he has always been a lover of the body of Christ. Dr. Wilson's book, *Understanding the New Birth*, is written in an easy-to-read, yet thought-provoking, manner. One of the things that I love most about this book is that it redirects the church back to the basics of the Christian faith. With the misdirection in the church today and the rapidly declining moral status within society, this work offers a very poignant and timely message for believers both old and new. I highly recommend this book!

Kervin J. Smith
President, Kervin J. Smith Ministries
Author of Living Single, Jezebel's Church,
Prophetic Power, *and* Body Building:
Getting the Church in Shape

Timeless integrity and sincerity describe this profound gentleman with a unique anointing on his life. Apostle Wilson is a man of God who has steadfastly endured trends, fads, and clichés. He stands as a testament to the church of Jesus Christ that truth will always outlast a trend. His book will be a blessing today and a revelatory tool for years. It will move the reader from faith to faith and glory to glory.

Apostle, Dr. Thomas H. Lounsbury
Lighthouse Ministries International

CONTENTS

FOREWORD

〜〜〜〜

One evening Jesus Christ had one of the most important dialogues that He ever had during His ministry with a man named Nicodemus. During that conversation, He unveiled a powerful revelation concerning the new birth. The first thing that He explained was in the form of a command. Jesus said to Nicodemus and to all humanity alike, "You must be born again!" There was very little room for discussion on that matter. In fact, it may have appeared that Jesus was acting a bit presumptuously or maybe even arrogantly.

To say to a person, "you must be" automatically infers that the person is lacking in a particular area. To command someone to be born again implies that his or her first birth was insufficient and needs to be repeated. It was pretty obvious that Jesus was not speaking to a stillborn child, expecting to raise it from the dead. Jesus was speaking to the untapped possibilities, potential, and purpose in Nicodemus.

In other words, Jesus was trying to convey a basic message to Nicodemus: You will never maximize who you are and become what you were ordained to be until you become born again. Although Nicodemus was a highly educated man, with numerous honors and designations, and although he was a highly respected Jewish leader, Jesus informed him that he would have to begin his life all over again, but this time the right way.

There are so many people in our society today that are in the same condition as Nicodemus was. You may believe, by all appearances, that you have what you need to survive, yet something is still missing. Everything that you've pursued in life tends to fall short of your expectations, leaving you still wanting. No matter how diligent you search in every other area to find peace, promise, and satisfaction, you will never be satisfied until you start over and begin again with Christ.

I hear a clarion cry from the Father for all sinners to begin again. He is also informing the church, which has become so lackadaisical in her faith and in her commitment to Him, to also begin again. What a grave danger it is to believe that you are alive when, in fact, you are really dead. Jesus Himself offered His body as a living sacrifice to enable those who were dead in their trespasses and sins to come into an abundant and eternal life, leaving no excuse for anyone to perish.

After Jesus voiced His command to Nicodemus, He then gave this very confused yet spiritually hungry man the how-to formula for receiving this born again experience. He said that being born again requires being born of the water and of the Spirit. To omit either of the two would invalidate the other. *Understanding the New Birth* details in a pragmatic style how to be born again by the water and the Spirit. It recapitulates the entire process by strategically pointing every person to the blood of Jesus, the sole factor for our salvation.

It is one thing to write about a topic from another person's point of view. But a topic takes on an entirely different level of potency when the person writing it has literally lived the message. Apostle John Wilson has lived this message. From the beginning of our God-ordained connection until this very moment, I have witnessed firsthand his unerring conviction to see souls saved. After more than forty-eight years of Christian ministry, his conviction has not wavered one bit.

If you truly desire to know more about the new birth in Christ Jesus, then I recommend that you devour the words on these pages, digest them, and then utilize them for the glory of the King. I believe that after you have read the text, you will have a greater appreciation and understanding of the new birth, but even more, you will be equipped to share what you have learned with others.

And there are three that bear witness on earth: the Spirit, the water, and the blood; and these three agree as one (1 John 5:8).

Apostle Cheryl Fortson
Senior Pastor
Full Gospel Foundation Building Ministries International
Bloomfield, Connecticut
Author of *That They May Be One in Christ*

Chapter One

WHAT DOES IT MEAN TO BE BORN AGAIN?

※◎◎◎◎◎◎

One of the things that have surprised me in my nearly forty-eight years of ministry is that many people that profess to be saved cannot clearly articulate what it actually means to be born again. It seems a bit strange that anyone who has been saved for any period of time would have difficulty in giving an explanation of his or her conversion experience. One of the reasons there has been so much misunderstanding is simply that Christian people, both learned and unlearned, have tag-teamed in an unending battle to confuse the very simple message of salvation in the name of Jesus.

My sincere intention and the reason that I wrote this work is to demystify this often misunderstood subject.

For the person who is already a professing believer, I would like this work to serve as a strength builder and an eye opener to some truths about the new birth that have been concealed from you. To the unbeliever, my hope is that you will walk away from this book a completely changed man or woman, boy or girl. I will attempt to answer all of the questions that you have asked and never received adequate answers for concerning salvation. It is one thing to know the answer for someone else to benefit from. But it is far more intimate when you know the answer for your own benefit.

There are literally dozens and dozens of relevant passages of scriptures that I could use to begin my course. However, I believe that it would be most befitting to begin with what I believe is the most appropriate text that deals specifically with this question. Although we will use various scriptures to explain the topic and to enrich your understanding, I will focus most of my efforts on the story of Nicodemus, a revered Jewish ruler. It was Nicodemus who became famous for asking the question that millions of people have asked since his time: "How can I be born again?"

That question is a loaded question since it has so many implications. It is really many questions in one. You know, you've probably been there if you are not at the point right now. You may have asked, "How can I be born again when I am so old?" "How can I be born again when I am so young?" "How can I be born again when I am so evil, when I am so sinful?" "How can I be born again when I feel so unloved?" "How can I be born again when I can't forgive myself for past failures?" These lists of questions could go on and on forever.

The real truth is that many people put restrictions on themselves and on God's ability to work through them. For the most part they allow the demons in their past to suffocate the angels and destiny in their future, staying stuck in the here and now and never moving forward as God intended for them. Do not worry. There is still hope. Nicodemus faced the same kind of dilemma that you may be facing, and he overcame it and you can too. So let's use as a model for this section Nicodemus' real-life encounter with God as recorded in the Gospel of John.

There was a man of the Pharisees named Nicodemus, a ruler of the Jews. This man came to Jesus by night and said to Him, "Rabbi, we know that You are a teacher come from God; for no one can do these signs that You do unless God is with him." Jesus answered and said to him, "Most assuredly, I say to you, unless one is born again, he cannot see the kingdom of God." Nicodemus said to Him, "How can a man be born when he is old? Can he enter a second time into his mother's womb and be born?" Jesus answered, "Most assuredly, I say to you, unless one is born of water and the Spirit, he cannot enter the kingdom of God. That which is born of the flesh is flesh, and that which is born of the Spirit is spirit. Do not marvel that I said to you, 'You must be born again.' The wind blows where it wishes, and you hear the sound of it, but cannot tell where it comes from and where it goes. So is everyone who is born of the Spirit." Nicodemus answered and said to Him, "How can these things be?" Jesus answered and said to him, "Are you the teacher of Israel, and do not know these things?" (John 3:1-10)

A Different Kind of Man or Woman

One of the things that we can first infer from these wonderful scriptures is that Nicodemus was truly a different kind of man. What does that mean and why is that important? The reason this is important is because you need to understand that God is looking for a different kind of man or woman.

"God is looking for a different kind of man or woman."

Contrary to what you might think, God is not looking for people that have it all together. In fact, I don't really know if those kinds of people really exist. The "having it all together" group of people are not real-life people but rather are people you will find in a make-believe fairy tale.

People that are real, the ones who bleed and cry and feel pain, are far from believing that they have all of their ducks in a row. To the contrary, most people feel as if they can never seem to get things just right. No matter how hard they try it still seems as if they can't do what they know they should be doing in life.

The reason for that is because we are all human and all humans are prone to failure. Some of those failures will be minor and some will be massive. The bottom line is that God does not look at our failures and insufficiencies as a reason to point the finger at us. The Apostle Paul put it this way:

> For I know that in me (that is, in my flesh) nothing good dwells; for to will is present with me, but how to perform what is good I do not find. For the good that I will to do, I do not do; but the evil I will not to do, that I practice. Now if I do what I will not to do, it is no longer I who do it, but sin that dwells in me. I find then a law, that evil is present with me, the one who wills to do good (Romans 7:18-21).

The dilemma that created a war in Paul's mind was actually a good thing in that it caused him to look to God as his constant helper and not to his flesh or human intellect. God is not looking for an opportunity to condemn us as some people falsely believe. God is looking for an opportunity to show us His power by taking the broken pieces of our shattered lives and putting them back together again. The only thing is that when we allow Him to do this we aren't restored back to our original state, but rather we are recreated into a masterpiece using the tattered, torn, raw materials within us.

For that reason God is looking for a different kind of man or woman. He's not looking for your average "Joe Christian" who acts, talks, and behaves like a brother or sister in the Lord. God is not looking for the stereotypical, conventional idea of a new convert. When I speak of conventional, I am talking about the brother or sister who has never gotten into any trouble in life. You know, the person who has never worried about anything more than a day. The in-control, in-command individual who constantly makes the right choices in life, yet the only thing that he or she is lacking is a real commitment to Jesus.

"It is our dirty little secrets that God wishes to redeem us from."

I guess it would be nice if everybody's story were as clean as that story reads. Unfortunately, most are not. At least they are not like that in the real world. The truth of the matter is that most people's stories are exactly the opposite. It's been said that most people in life have a dirty little secret that they don't want anyone to know. And it is our dirty little secrets that God wishes to redeem us from.

Plainly put and contrary to most church members' passions, God is consistently searching for people that have serious issues. Although many believers can be pompous and scornful towards people that are in greater need than they are, God is searching for the people that everyone else has given up on. I call these people the same thing that God calls them: different people.

Take a good look at this list of different people and see if you can find yourself in one or more places on this list.

What Does It Mean to Be Born Again?

One Who Had an Abortion	Drug User	Manic Depressive
Drug Dealer	Murderer	Thief
Compulsive Liar	Fornicator	Terrorist
White-collar Criminal	Bipolar	Child Abuser
Woman Beater	Racist	Embezzler
Con-artist	Extortionist	Schizophrenic
Incest Victim	Adulterer	Deadbeat Dad

If you can personally identify with one or more of these categories, then you are the different kind of person that God is looking for. God is neither afraid of you nor is He trying to avoid you because you may be somewhat different from the next person. He looks at your different life as a challenge. He desires for you to become transformed by His power. Nicodemus was a different kind of man. He wasn't as involved in sinful indulgences such as the ones listed above. In fact, he was a strict and devout Jew. To the best of his ability, he followed all of the Law, observed the Sabbath, and prayed daily.

You might ask, "What then qualifies such an honorable man to be on this list?" Although this man had obvious merit and good standing in his community, Nicodemus was a part of a group of people that vehemently opposed Jesus. They were called the Pharisees.

Consider what it's like being a good guy who belongs to a notorious gang such as the Mafia, or a hate group such as the Aryan Nation, or some other kind of underground, organized criminal group. I realize that may sound like an oxymoron trying to combine these totally different descriptions, but this was the case with Nicodemus. The Pharisees posed as the spiritually elite within the society that existed during Jesus' time.

However, they were not really spiritual at all, but were merely religious. And there is a distinct difference between being spiritual and being religious. Religion is basically adhering to a set of rules and regulations to please man. Spirituality, the biblical way, is breaking all the rules to pursue God passionately. Spirituality is following hard after God. The Pharisees had a form of godliness but they denied God's power. Despite the countless records of Jesus' healings and miracle-working feats, they continued to deny and ignore the truth and the unmistakable reality of His power. It was to this highly critical group that Nicodemus belonged.

The Scriptures refer to Nicodemus as *"a ruler of the Jews"* (John 3:1). Nicodemus was not necessarily a government official. But he was a respected leader in terms of Judaic education. Although he was a learned man, Nicodemus was not like those who only believed intellectually. He was clearly different from the others. He went far beyond mere intellectualism. He was moved in his conscience and felt a thirst and hunger in his soul. This led him to have a profound attraction to the miraculous works that Jesus performed.

8

What Does It Mean to Be Born Again?

Although he did not fully understand how, he believed that Jesus was somehow connected with the coming Kingdom that had been spoken of by the prophets in prior times. Little did he even realize that Jesus would neither shun nor scorn him but instead would be open to his unique differences. In the same way that Christ offered grace to Nicodemus, He will warmly receive you too, despite your unique differences. Despite his obvious disparities, Nicodemus knew through his yearning soul that Jesus, in spite of His differences, was no ordinary man, but rather a man of mysteriously divine substance.

And had no need that anyone should testify of man, for He knew what was in man (John 2:25).

He Had It All—or Did He?

From an outsider's point of view, it appeared as though Nicodemus had everything that he desired in life. Based on John 19:39, which states, *"And Nicodemus, who at first came to Jesus by night, also came, bringing a mixture of myrrh and aloes, about a hundred pounds,"* one can conclude that Nicodemus must have been a wealthy man. Only the wealthy in the society during that time could afford to lavish Jesus with such expensive gifts. Not only were the aloes and myrrh pricey commodities, but Nicodemus came with nearly one hundred pounds of these medicinal plants and sweet fragrances, a gift worthy of mentioning.

Giving such a lofty gift would not only identify him as rich, but *very* rich. Added to his wealth, he was also a member in good standing of the Sanhedrin council, which was a group of leaders from the ancient Jewish nation comprised of seventy to seventy-two members that made rulings in civil and criminal matters. The Sanhedrin council was very selective about who they allowed to enter into their ranks. Because of that, they proceeded with great caution in their selection process, only choosing men who had already proven to have an influential track record.

True, Nicodemus was a man of great influence and wealth, but he was also a man of remarkable intellectual acumen. The members of the Sanhedrin were great defenders of the written Jewish laws. They were required to be able to quote the law from memory. They also were required to be able to interpret each detail of the law and thoroughly explain it at a moment's notice. Not just anyone could remember such mass amounts of information. This kind of memorization took a special kind of person. Only a person who was skilled in the art of thinking and open to the vast world of higher learning could qualify for such an arduous undertaking.

Just glancing over Nicodemus' lofty résumé and past achievements proves that he had much going for him. Despite all of the things that he had, all the fineries and trappings that followed the lives of people of such noble distinction, he still did not have enough to satisfy his hungry soul. And that is precisely why he began to seek Christ out, like a night stalker would seek out his prey. His curiosity about the living Lord continued to grow rapidly. He wanted to know a little bit about everything concerning Jesus.

He wanted to know exactly how Jesus resurrected people from the dead. His curiosity drove him into a quandary. He pondered questions such as, "How does He heal the sick?" "How does He cause blind eyes to open?" "My friend could not walk since birth, but after his encounter with Jesus, he miraculously began walking again. How does He do it?" Nicodemus was fascinated by the many miracles that Jesus performed. However, there was nothing that would fill his interest more than receiving a concrete understanding on the new birth. Although he did not understand just how Jesus performed His healings and miracles, Nicodemus, like many of his colleagues, came to accept the healings and miracles as frequently seen aspects of Jesus' ministry. There were, after all, other people during this era that performed various tricks and produced amazing miracles using witchcraft and sorcery. So, Jesus was somehow placed in this category of magi. However, Nicodemus knew there was one thing that only God Himself could ever have the capability of doing and that was forgiving men and women from sin. In this area of forgiving humankind's sin, God had no contemporaries or equals. The very thought of someone claiming to have the power to forgive made Nicodemus much desirous to know Jesus more intimately.

Many years ago, I remember how churches would have members routinely organize door-to-door evangelizing campaigns, trying to get people saved and convincing them to join the local church. Most of these door-to-door evangelists then (and perhaps some still do this today) would instinctively go to the absolute worst areas of town to witness. They would go to the poorest of the poor with the message of Christ's love and forgiveness. They would often use the words of Jesus to justify their honest intentions.

Jesus said:

The Spirit of the LORD is upon Me, because He has anointed Me to preach the gospel to the poor; He has sent Me to heal the brokenhearted, to proclaim liberty to the captives and recovery of sight to the blind, to set at liberty those who are oppressed; to proclaim the acceptable year of the LORD (Luke 4:18-19).

They would say, "Jesus commanded us to preach to the poor and that is exactly what we intend to do." They would never go into areas where the rich lived, the up and outers. In fact many of them felt strongly intimidated by people that were recognized in society for their honorable deeds or for their contributions in the areas of commerce, education, and the arts. They would only feel comfortable witnessing to people that lived in the housing projects, government-owned property. In some ways, this made the person who was witnessing feel good, knowing that he or she was obviously better off than the needy person hearing the message was.

Most of this witnessing bunch from yesteryear would never feel a stirring of the Spirit of God to reach out to the rich lost. They would even go as far to defend their neglectful actions as to quote the Bible verse which says, *"For it is easier for a camel to go through the eye of a needle than for a rich man to enter the kingdom of God"* (Luke 18:25). They would argue that since getting to heaven was so difficult for men and women of financial wealth anyway, it did not make much sense to waste energy trying to share Christ's message with them. They thought it would be far better to minister to the poor since they would gravitate to the message far more quickly.

Although the latter statement may be true, it is not true that rich people cannot receive salvation. Nor is it true that a rich person is more inherently lost than a poor one, or that he or she has less of a chance of receiving salvation than a poor sinner does. The poor generally have fewer options in life than a rich person, and because of that, they will be more able to give their undivided attention to the Gospel message. However, there is nowhere in the entire Bible that justifies believers freeing themselves from reaching out to people of worth.

Nicodemus' story perfectly fits within the scenario I've described. Had he been included in our modern culture, he would have lived in the finest subdivision. He would have dined at the most exquisite restaurants. He would have had an annual subscription to the most prestigious golfing, racquetball, and yacht clubs in the world. Yes, he would boast a six-figure income, perhaps as much as a quarter-million dollars annual income. Despite all of these material things, he would still be in lack of something far greater than material things—Jesus.

Many people today are in the same predicament as Nicodemus. They seem to have it all on the surface.

They are esteemed within society for all of their accomplishments and honorable achievements. Lack of money is not their problem. They have plenty of money, plenty of real estate, plenty of gold and silver, and unquestionable influence and power. However, without Jesus, one can have all of those things and yet still feel as though one has nothing at all. What a shame! What a crime, to have so much, having worked so hard to earn it and still not be fulfilled. The rich and the poor have this one thing in common—they both need Jesus.

"The rich and the poor have one thing in common—they both need Jesus."

The rich and the poor have this in common, the LORD is the maker of them all (Proverbs 22:2).

There is one who makes himself rich, yet has nothing; and one who makes himself poor, yet has great riches (Proverbs 13:7).

Now Is the Right Time

There have been long debates concerning when the right time actually is for a person to come to Jesus. Is there really such a thing as the right time? The Bible offers the concept of predestination. The Apostle Paul, in the book of Romans, suggests that every person created by God was and is predestined to be saved.

14

What Does It Mean to Be Born Again?

For whom He foreknew, He also predestined to be conformed to the image of His Son, that He might be the firstborn among many brethren. Moreover whom He predestined, these He also called; whom He called, these He also justified; and whom He justified, these He also glorified (Romans 8:29-30).

This basically tells us that every person was called to be like Jesus. In fact, that is a good way of looking at salvation. Salvation is our journey to becoming more and more like Jesus. It is being conformed and molded into the image of God. Salvation begins when you confess His lordship and believe in the finished work of Christ.

Some people falsely believe that since this is so, there is no real need for the unbeliever to acknowledge their sin to God asking for forgiveness. They believe that they'll automatically be forgiven without any involvement on their part. This teaching causes many people to foolishly believe that they have all the time in the world to make the decision to follow Jesus. They are in no hurry to accept the finished work of Jesus. Unbeknown to them, this is the very place that the devil wants them to be—in the place of ignorance. He wants to keep them ignorant of the *truth*, which is the only vehicle that can free humanity. The real truth is that you should never put off a decision to follow Jesus. Tomorrow is not promised to you. Just knowing that should make you eager to seize the moment.

In the Old Testament, Joshua made it clear that we should choose the Lord now and not later.·

And if it seems evil to you to serve the LORD, choose for yourselves this day whom you will serve, whether the gods which your fathers served that were on the other side of the River, or the gods of the Amorites, in whose land you dwell. But as for me and my house, we will serve the LORD (Joshua 24:15).

Nicodemus chose the nighttime to come to Jesus. He knew that the night would be far safer to come to Jesus because he realized that his colleagues and peers would be watching his every move during the daylight. Because of his high standing in society, if he had been caught pursuing Jesus and asking probing questions, he would have been ostracized, expelled from his religious order, and possibly even stoned. Yet none of those things stopped him from getting the answers that he so desperately wanted from God. For Nicodemus, the present was the right time.

"You should never put off a decision to follow Jesus."

Nicodemus (he who came to Jesus by night, being one of them) said to them, "Does our law judge a man before it hears him and knows what he is doing?" (John 7:50-52)

And Nicodemus, who at first came to Jesus by night, also came, bringing a mixture of myrrh and aloes, about a hundred pounds (John 19:39).

What Does It Mean to Be Born Again?

Salvation is now! Far too many people make lame excuses for why they won't accept Jesus now. Over my many years in ministry, I may not have heard every single excuse, but I have sure come close. The enemy wants to get people totally distracted long enough for them to lose out on a free deal. Just because salvation is available does not mean that the offer will last forever. Salvation does have a time of expiration. There will come a time when, after repeated rejections of the Holy Spirit's prompting, God's Spirit will no longer work with you.

And the LORD said, "My Spirit shall not strive with man forever, for he is indeed flesh; yet his days shall be one hundred and twenty years" (Genesis 6:3).

One of the ways that I believe you can overcome the spirit of procrastination or help others who need salvation to overcome the spirit of procrastination is simply to combat the list of diversions that the enemy sends your way in the form of meaningless excuses. Below I have listed some of the most ridiculous excuses that I have heard of why people put off accepting Jesus. Often we just don't realize how foolish we may sound to others since we really are not hearing ourselves.

For this reason, if you see any excuses on this list that you have said, or heard another person say, I ask you to totally eradicate the phrase from your daily conversation forever. By doing this, you will begin to free yourself from all of the dross that so rapidly fills your soul and that causes you to become insensitive and unhearing to the voice of the Lord.

Reasons people put off being saved:

- I'm just not ready.

- I don't want to be a hypocrite.

- If I get saved in front of the church they are going to embarrass me, and I don't want to be embarrassed in front of people.

- I am waiting to get my life together first. Once I clean myself up, then I'll get saved.

- I'm too young.

- I'm too old.

- I don't want get saved until my spouse gets saved with me. We planned on doing this together.

- When my boyfriend (girlfriend) comes to church with me, then I'll get saved.

- If I get saved, I can't have fun anymore.

- I don't really believe that I can be forgiven from all of the negative things that I have done.

If you've ever uttered any of these reasons why you have put off salvation, I want you to know that none of them are good enough. There are no valid reasons for putting off salvation. You are never too young or too old to get saved. You can get saved as early on as you are able to understand the message of salvation. God still saves the older people also. You may have seen people at various churches do some silly things and outright embarrass people. But in all actuality, you really don't have to get saved in a church at all. You can receive Christ right where you are now, at this moment. So even that is an illegitimate excuse.

Don't wait for a spouse, a boyfriend, or a girlfriend to make a decision for you that you should be making for yourself. Where you spend eternity should be solely your choice and should never be left up to your lover. If your spouse or lover really loves you, they would encourage you to make the right step forward toward

"There are no valid reasons for putting off salvation."

Jesus whether they decide to follow or not. And the one about being a hypocrite has become so old, tired, and worn out. If you don't want to be a hypocrite, then don't be one. It's really that simple. A hypocrite is nothing more than a person who pretends to be something he or she is really not. A hypocrite is much like our modern day actors. You may have seen one of your favorite actors portraying the role of an alcoholic, a racist, a drug abuser, or a violent murderer. Yet, in real life these people are not any of those things. They are only portraying a role. In a sense, they are hypocrites.

If you want to be saved, then simply receive Christ. You ask, "Well, what if I mess up? What if I make a mistake? Won't I then be considered a hypocrite?" No, you'll be considered a child of God who is prone to failure and needs to be instructed on how to position yourself not to fall. After all, there is very little that you can do in your own strength and power to keep yourself from falling anyway. Only God Almighty has the power to keep you from falling. And only as you look to Him to supply all of your needs can you actually understand what it really means to be saved. True salvation is total reliance on God and zero reliance on your flesh.

Now unto him that is able to keep you from falling, and to present you faultless before the presence of his glory with exceeding joy, to the only wise God our Saviour, be glory and majesty, dominion and power, both now and for ever. Amen (Jude 24-25 KJV).

No Matter Who You Are, You Can Be Changed

And I thank Christ Jesus our Lord who has enabled me, because He counted me faithful, putting me into the ministry, although I was formerly a blasphemer, a persecutor, and an insolent man; but I obtained mercy because I did it ignorantly in unbelief. And the grace of our Lord was exceedingly abundant, with faith and love which are in Christ Jesus. This is a faithful saying and worthy of all acceptance, that Christ Jesus came into the world to save sinners, of whom I am chief. However, for this reason I obtained mercy, that in me first Jesus Christ might show all longsuffering, as a pattern to those who are going to believe on Him for everlasting life (1 Timothy 1:12-16).

There is something that you must understand and that is this: No matter how bad you think you are, you can change if you want to. There is no sinner on earth that is so sinful that the blood of Jesus cannot save that person. I've heard people boast about the many different sins that they have dabbled in. Some have said things to me like, "I've got to be the worst sinner on earth. You really don't want me to come to your church." "If I do, the roof might cave in." "Everybody might get struck by lightning. God's after me, Pastor." Although some people actually believe these statements, nothing could be further from the truth. No matter how bad you are, you are probably not worse than the Apostle Paul was prior to his conversion.

Paul was called the chief of sinners. Can you actually be called the chief of sinners? What is a chief? A *chief* is the head or leader of a group of men or women. So Paul, in exclaiming this bold confession, is actually letting us know that he was not only a great sinner but also a trained, mobilized, and deployed sinner, commissioned to do evil deeds. He was a commander of sinners, yet God saved him. If you are not convinced, allow me to enlighten you just a bit on just how notorious Paul actually was.

And they stoned Stephen as he was calling on God and saying, "Lord Jesus, receive my spirit." Then he knelt down and cried out with a loud voice, "Lord, do not charge them with this sin." And when he had said this, he fell asleep (Acts 7:59-60).

Now **Saul was consenting to his death.** *At that time a great persecution arose against the church which was at Jerusalem; and they were*

21

all scattered throughout the regions of Judea and Samaria, except the apostles. And devout men carried Stephen to his burial, and made great lamentation over him. As for Saul, he made havoc of the church, entering every house, and dragging off men and women, committing them to prison (Acts 8:1-3, emphasis mine).

Then **Saul, still breathing threats and murder against the disciples of the Lord,** *went to the high priest and asked letters from him to the synagogues of Damascus,* **so that if he found any who were of the Way, whether men or women, he might bring them bound** *to Jerusalem* (Acts 9:1-2, emphasis mine).

At that time, since he was the chief of sinners, Saul, who would later become known as Paul the apostle after his conversion, would give his chiefly authorization for his followers to stone people to death. Stephen was the first martyr to die the death of such violent opposition for the sake of Christ and His Kingdom. Could you imagine what it would be like if you were literally stoned to death? Just thinking about the experience and not even feeling the literal stoning is painful all by itself. The act of stoning any human being or any living thing for that matter is tantamount to the most horrible criminal act. It proved that he was heartless, grossly insensitive, callous, inhumane, and barbaric. Yet Saul, later to become the Apostle Paul, was instrumental in ordering not one, but several executions of innocent people.

Added to that, Saul intentionally tried to destroy the church. He caused havoc in worship services that were in progress. Beyond that he bred great fear among Christians by threatening their lives everywhere they went. He did not have any respect toward those whom he would persecute. If they believed Jesus' name, they automatically became qualified targets for maltreatment and possible murder. He persecuted and killed men, women, and small children. He was a cold, merciless murderer. The strange thing is that he never considered his actions to be totally ungodly and unjust, being the practicing Jew that he was.

Despite his terrible track record and negative past, Jesus still made room for this man in the Kingdom of God. After his conversion and name change, Paul went on to write nearly two-thirds of the New Testament, was one of the greatest missionaries, helped to organize the early church, and was imprisoned for the sake of the Lord for more than five years. How did a man so notorious and evil suddenly become changed? He was changed only by God's power.

In our modern, religious culture, most laity and clergy would have voted to give Paul the death penalty, leaving him without an option for salvation. That is not how God sees things. God will take the vilest of sinners, the chief, if you will, and turn him or her into a saint. So you thought you were so bad. Think again. If you think that your sins are far too much for our Lord to deal with, then you are wrong. No one's sins are so heavy that they outweigh the power of the shed blood of the Lord Jesus Christ.

"God will take the vilest of sinners and turn him or her into a saint."

I don't care what you have done in the past or what you are doing in the present. None of those things really matter. You can be changed if you choose to believe that you can. The only thing that separates you from receiving your salvation is your belief in the only God who can save you. If you can believe it, you can truly receive it. And I stand in total agreement with you.

Again I say to you that if two of you agree on earth concerning anything that they ask, it will be done for them by My Father in heaven. For where two or three are gathered together in My name, I am there in the midst of them (Matthew 18:19-20).

Chapter Two

HOW CAN I BE BORN AGAIN? (PART ONE)

≈≈≈≈

In this chapter, I want to explain the way you can be born again. There is absolutely no sense in talking about the new birth without providing you with the means to receive it. As I was growing up in the holiness church, I saw many sincere people witness to others about the message of salvation through Jesus. When those potential believers would come to our church and receive Christ, these unassuming people often would be put through a series of motions just to get saved.

They would be asked to repeat a whole bunch of things over and over again before they were considered saved. For one, they would have to confess their sins, then beg God to forgive them for those sins. In some ways, it seemed to me as if they were sort of taking a big gamble. Some seemed to think, "I need to be for-given from my sins, and I would like to have a proper relationship with God, so let me do everything in my flesh to receive His attention, then maybe God just might save me. If He doesn't, then I still haven't lost much, so it really doesn't matter." Or so they thought.

"God never intended the plan of salvation to be difficult."

Many of them believed that whether God could save them or not was as much a gamble as a novice poker player betting his last five thousand dollars on a Foxwoods table. Although it was a common sight to see, I knew deep down inside that God's plan for salvation was not as tedious and labor intensive as they were making it out to be. As I began to grow in the things of God, I realized that although those wonderful, senior Christians sincerely gave their all in helping people understand God's plan for salvation, they simultaneously confused them.

Unfortunately because of this introduction to the Christian faith, confused is exactly where most of these people remained concerning salvation. It's my inten-tion to remove the confusion, clearing the pathway to the Savior. What I want you to understand is that God never intended the plan of salvation to be difficult in the first place. He wanted to make salvation as easy as learning one-two-three. The reason why the plan does not seem that simple is because religious people over the years have complicated the Word of God to keep their own personal traditions alive. They began to honor their traditions more than they honored God and far more than they cared about people.

Making the word of God of no effect through your tradition which you have handed down. And many such things you do (Mark 7:13).

Although being born again has far greater implications than being saved from sin, I would like to use both phrases interchangeably for the sake of this work. And because it is my goal to help usher people into a born-again experience with Jesus, I will use both terms (being saved and being born again) hand in hand as to create the vehicle that will cause you to arrive at God's ultimate place for you. For the sake of clarity, I want you to understand that when we hear the word *saved,* we picture the concept of being saved from our sins and ultimately from eternal destruction.

On the other hand, being born again tends to suggest that we experienced a formal dying to our old self, necessitating the need to be born anew. When we are born again, we are born to new realities. The old ways that we used to think and to know are null and void. Our behavior changes, our perspective on life changes, the ways we view God and His people suddenly change.

However, some people don't quite make it to this level of spiritual consciousness. This is one of the main reasons why so many believers don't realize their salvation potential and never fulfill their prospective purposes in life. Far too few ever realize and actualize the type of lifestyle that God intended them to live. My intent is to show you exactly how other people in the Bible received or arrived at the point of their new birth and how you can too, if you have not done so already. The goal is not merely being saved from destruction, as the doomsayers so dogmatically preach. My goal is to safely escort you into the zoë, or life, where prosperity and the peace of God kiss one another and become one.

Salvation Is in Your Mouth

But what does it say? "The word is near you, in your mouth and in your heart" (that is, the word of faith which we preach): that if you confess with your mouth the Lord Jesus and believe in your heart that God has raised Him from the dead, you will be saved. For with the heart one believes unto righteousness, and with the mouth confession is made unto salvation (Romans 10:8-10).

One of the first things that I would like you to understand about salvation is that it is not far from you. Throughout the course of my ministry God has allowed me to touch multiple thousands of lives over the years. Many have been born again. However, many others failed to realize how close in terms of proximity their salvation really was. Because of ultra-traditional religion (meaning religious rituals that have become powerless over time), most people started to believe that God was far from their reach. They viewed God as an extraterrestrial being incapable of being contacted by humans. Nothing could be further from the truth.

Years ago, there was a slogan or phrase that used to be said: "If God seems far away, then who moved?" The point is that God has always desired to have an intimate relationship with His creation. He went to great lengths to redeem us back to the Father. So the issue isn't really whether or not God will hear you when you call on Him, but rather when will you call on Him?

> *"God has always desired to have an intimate relationship with His creation."*

Everybody seems to have preconceived notions about God's ability to communicate with us, as well as our ability to communicate with Him. Some believe that God only hears the voice of the so-called spiritually elite, but not the sinner crying out. You may have thought, "I am not a priest, a pastor, an apostle, a prophet, or a social dignitary. If I don't serve in any of those capacities, then how can I have easy access to an Almighty God?" Your access is in your mouth!

Book publishers have produced literally millions of books and several thousands of titles about the power of words, the power of the tongue, and the power of positive confession. Despite all of the books written on the subject, people still tend to get a bit tongue-tied when it actually comes to putting their knowledge into practice. But unless you practice what you know, you will never have anything in life. Faith begins with speaking aloud what you believe. For all intents and purposes, you are right now the totality of everything that you have been confessing about yourself throughout the course of your life.

I teach my parishioners to avoid using words that will ultimately run blessings away from themselves. Don't say, "I'm broke. I am sick as a dog. I can't help it and I'll never be." Words like these tend to create our negative world. What you confess will come to you. According to Romans 10:8-10, the word you so desperately need in order to complete your change—the word of faith—is right in your mouth. All you have to do is confess with your mouth the lordship of Jesus Christ, believe what you've confessed, and then you will be saved.

Interestingly, the Bible makes it clear that you have to believe what you say in order to receive your salvation. There are so many people that say a whole lot of different things, yet they really don't believe what they are saying. You have to speak words of power. When I speak of words that produce powerful results in your life, they are not just a bunch of empty expressions. They are words that you believe beyond any doubt. Think about it this way…if you don't believe your own words, why should anyone else? Why should God believe you?

When you ask God to save you, to forgive you, and to deliver you from the bondage of sin, you have to believe that He will do exactly what you've asked. It is somewhat senseless to ask if you are not going to believe. But if you ask believing, the powerful force behind that combination will cause all of the devils in hell and on earth to tremble because they know that you are moments away from receiving God's mercy, grace, and power.

So, you really don't have to find God by looking into the deep and mysterious things. You don't have to stare all day long at the skies hoping to receive a supernatural revelation concerning your salvation. If those things happen for you that is fine. But if they don't, there is still hope. You can still enjoy the kind of God-to-man connection that you've always dreamed about but didn't know how to make happen. God is no respecter of persons. This means He doesn't love any one of us more than the rest. He loves us all equally. He will save the drunken man in the alley just as rapidly as He will save a Wall Street investor that is strung out on avarice and greed. He will save the drug dealer and simultaneously save the drug addict. It does not matter who you are. But it does matter what you say. God responds to our faith. And when you open up your mouth and confess Jesus as Lord you have taken the very first steps to activating your spiritual inheritance. Again it does not matter who you are; it only matters what you say.

For "whoever calls on the name of the LORD shall be saved" (Romans 10:13).

The Right Spirit

Let's look at this text again:

Jesus answered, "Most assuredly, I say to you, unless one is born of water and the Spirit, he cannot enter the kingdom of God. That which is born of the flesh is flesh, and that which is born of the Spirit is spirit. Do not marvel that I said to you, 'You must be born again.' The wind blows where it wishes, and you hear the sound of it, but cannot tell where it comes from and where it goes. So is everyone who is born of the Spirit." Nicodemus answered and said to Him, "How can these things be?" (John 3:5-9)

In this text we see a few things happening. Jesus and Nicodemus are having a face-to-face conversation. Jesus is coming into contact with humanity while, on the other hand, Nicodemus is discovering Deity for the very first time. In some ways they are alike, and in some ways they are different. It is true that they are both men. However, they are not like just any other man. Jesus is the Son of God, yet Nicodemus is the son of a natural man. They were both fathered, yet the Holy Spirit, not a natural man, fathered Jesus.

Nicodemus was a very devout and religious person. Despite all of his religious acts and convictions, he was not a child of God. So for the most part, he had religion, but he did not possess salvation. Having not known who God really was, he was greatly shocked to learn that his religion, which he so faithfully practiced and ascribed to, was not sufficient. Like many people both then and now, he thought that having good, old-time religion meant having it all. Old-time religion, as good as it sounds, is not God's desired goal for His creation.

Create in me a clean heart, O God, and renew a steadfast spirit within me (Psalm 51:10).

God wants to have a fresh and continuously renewed relationship with His people. God knows very well that old-time religion often carries with it the stench of decaying flesh, seeking to assassinate anything that would make it relevant to modern society. The "Old-Time-Religion Group" cares most about what God did in the past, not about what God is doing in the present. Nicodemus was religious, but not spiritual. He had a form of righteousness, yet he possessed an erroneous spirit.

> *"Old-time religion is not God's desired goal for His creation."*

There are many people that profess to be saved, yet they have a wrong spirit. They know how to go through all of the motions that "church folks" tend to go through. They know exactly when to lift their hands, how to hold their hands in a cup-like fashion, and when to cry. Instinctively they know when to shout and dance without needing a cue from the Hammond B-3 organ or from any of the praise band members. They know how to do what looks religious, yet for many of them, their spirit is not right.

God is not really concerned if you can't correctly do all of the things that appear to be "churchy." God is concerned about your having the right spirit. Although Nicodemus did not know Jesus intimately, he did know of Him from passing conversations around him. Most folks that I meet do not know former President William Jefferson Clinton or President George Bush personally, yet they have formed an opinion about these men based on what they've heard, regardless of whether the statements were true, false, or indifferent.

The point is that we often learn about people by hearing about them. That is exactly how Nicodemus gathered his information about Jesus, through hearing conversations. Obviously these conversations caused him to have a profound interest in, heightened curiosity about, and an undisclosed respect for Jesus. We can infer that he must have had respect for Jesus simply by how he addressed Jesus. He intentionally addressed Jesus as *"a teacher come from God"* (John 3:2).

Few, if any, of the other Jewish leaders of his day would have actually referred to Jesus in this manner. Many of them regularly hurled insults and false accusations against Jesus. Jesus was on the Jewish leaders' hit list in nearly every town that He visited. It was no secret that they wanted to kill Him. Despite all of the negative publicity that Jesus continuously received, Nicodemus still properly and respectfully addressed Jesus when speaking to Him.

Even though Nicodemus did not know Jesus personally, Jesus knew him for He knows all men. He is an omniscient, all-knowing Savior. Although it appeared from Nicodemus' questions that he was looking for a teacher, Jesus knew, by the Spirit, what he really needed more than anything. He knew that Nicodemus needed more than a mere teacher; he'd had many teachers throughout the course of his lifetime. What he needed was a Savior. He needed more than religion could ever offer. He needed to be regenerated. Nicodemus needed more than adherence to the law—he needed true life.

For Nicodemus to change was no small thing. He was considered a master in Israel. In many cases, he proudly wore that title. Quite honestly, he really was not qualified to wear such a lofty title. To look at him from the outside, it would appear that this title was befitting for him. For you see, the label had gone on, but the quality had not gone in. And those who wear and parade labels, yet do not have the goods on the inside, often prove that they do not have the right spirit.

Nicodemus did not have the right spirit. What I want you to know is that every person in the body of Christ should be far more concerned with possessing the right spirit than anything else. Having the right spirit directly correlates to your salvation experience. I have seen this problem of "having an improper spirit" even within the hierarchy of the universal church. Like Nicodemus, there are many people that profess to be saved, yet in all reality have never experienced the new birth.

Many of these precious yet uninformed people hold positions and titles in the church, which automatically leads us to believe that their dedication and consecration before God is truly authentic. But after a close and careful examination of their regular behavioral patterns, they are quickly revealed to be something other than what they seem. They serve the Lord with their lips by going through all of the motions. These motions make them appear to be really dedicated and church savvy, yet their hearts are far from him.

> *Hypocrites! Well did Isaiah prophesy about you, saying: "These people draw near to Me with their mouth, and honor Me with their lips, but their heart is far from Me. And in vain they worship Me, teaching as doctrines the commandments of men"* (Matthew 15:7-9).

You see, when a person has experienced the new birth, when he has truly been born again, every part of his personality undergoes a drastic change. We are not born again in sections or in parts, but the new birth involves the total person. Your attitudes change and your language changes. Even your conversation changes. Being truly born again involves a complete makeover of your whole spirit man. When you receive the right spirit, your activities, your habits, your conduct, and your very lifestyle change.

For example, when you are born again and get the right spirit, you can no longer harbor hate in your heart toward a person. The spirit of hate will supernaturally change to love. The Bible says, *"We know that we have passed from death to life, because we love the brethren. He who does not love his brother abides in death. Whoever hates his brother is a murderer, and you know that no murderer has eternal life abiding in him"* (1 John 3:14-15).

How Can I Be Born Again? (Part One)

This scripture is very interesting because it gives a major clue concerning the process of transformation. It shows us what actually happens to people when they transform from having the wrong spirit to having the right spirit. One of the very first things we see that marks a genuine salvation experience is a love for God's creation. You cannot truly be born again, yet walk around hating people and refusing to forgive them. There are people in the church that try to justify why they don't want to love this person or that person. They'll say, "She did me wrong two years ago," or "I never did like that brother." That kind of behavior is just not godly. When you get born again the spirit of God replaces your old spirit. When that happens, you become totally obsessed to love people. You become so grateful for the salvation that God allowed you to partake in that you just can't see yourself being judgmental toward anyone. Your mind thinks, "If God saved me from sin and unrighteousness, then He can surely save anybody." Thinking anything less than that is tantamount to being proud and arrogant.

It is prideful to believe that you are so wonderful and special that you did God a favor by coming to Him. We do no favors for God when we come to Him but rather we do ourselves the greatest favor knowing that if it weren't for His wonderful grace and matchless mercy, we too would be perishing with the vilest sinner on earth. Knowing that alone should make you love even the most unlovable person.

New Birth or Stillbirth?

The conversation that I mentioned earlier between Nicodemus and Jesus all began when this high-ranking ruler of the Jews went to Jesus as a representative of the Sanhedrin council. The council was disturbed about the miracles Jesus was performing. They knew He had some divine connection, but they had no information concerning His doctrine. Now Nicodemus was sent to question Jesus in order to take the information back to the council, so they would know how to deal with Jesus.

It was obvious that he admired Jesus. Instead of dealing with this business matter in the open, he chose to approach Jesus by night. He must have realized that his chances of being identified at night were far less than in broad daylight. So he chose the nighttime so as not to blow his cover. He had some personal, spiritual questions to ask Jesus, since his soul was hungry and longing for more than religion could offer. Nicodemus said to Jesus, *"Rabbi, we know that You are a teacher come from God; for no one can do these signs that You do unless God is with him"* (John 3:2).

Nicodemus was admitting that there were among them some that had the power to perform trickery, but the tricksters were unable to restore sight to the blind. These others could not defy the law of gravity by walking on the water. The council was investigating whether or not Jesus' work was ordained and sanctioned by God. Jesus knew what Nicodemus was trying to accomplish. So He said, "Nicodemus, I want you to know that except a man be born again, he cannot see the Kingdom of God" (see John 3:3).

How Can I Be Born Again? (Part One)

At this time Nicodemus revealed that he was spiritually retarded, for he asked a remedial question, *"How can a man be born when he is old? Can he enter a second time into his mother's womb and be born?"* (John 3:4) Jesus told him that they were talking about two different kinds of births. And even if it were possible for him to re-enter his mother's womb and be born again, he would still come out a sinner. That which is born of the flesh is flesh. That which is born of the spirit is spirit, and the spirit will never change.

Nicodemus could not understand the rationale of a new birth. His finite mind could only conceive a physical birth. He pictured a man or woman being born again by going back into the mother's womb, rather than by moving forward toward the spirit. Little did he realize...going backward would have only produced death, not life. It would have produced a stillborn child.

Unfortunately, the church at large has produced multitudes of "stillborn children." They have all of the appearances and appendages that are visible on children. These stillbirths have identifiable faces. They also have arms, legs, feet, hands, mouths, noses, lungs, hearts, kidneys, and even skin. They have everything that any healthy child possesses, except for one thing—they do not have the breath of God. It is not until one receives the breath of the living God that he or she comes alive. So it is really unimportant to merely look the part like Nicodemus did.

You will be identified clearly as a son or daughter of God when you breathe like He breathes. When your life resembles the life of Christ, you will know for sure that you have truly been born again. Right now, wherever you are, just ask the Holy Spirit to breathe on you and make you come alive in Jesus' name.

And the LORD God formed man of the dust of the ground, and breathed into his nostrils the breath of life; and man became a living being (Genesis 2:7).

Four Differences between the Two Births

Jesus took time and pointed out four dissimilarities in the two births.

That which the Flesh Produces vs.   **The New Birth**

Produces an old, sinful nature. King David said, *"Behold, I was shapen in iniquity; and in sin did my mother conceive me"* (Psalm 51:5 KJV).	Produces a righteous nature. *"For he hath made him to be sin for us, who knew no sin; that we might be made the righteousness of God in him"* (2 Corinthians 5:21 KJV).
Produces a corruptible nature. *"Being born again, not of corruptible seed, but of incorruptible, by the word of God, which liveth and abideth for ever"* (1 Peter 1:23 KJV).	Produces a nature that cannot sin. *"For his seed remaineth in him: and he cannot sin, because he is born of God"* (1 John 3:9b KJV).

Produces an old nature under the sentence of death. *"For the wages of sin is death, but the gift of God is eternal life..."* (Romans 6:23).	Produces a new nature under the new court ruling: life forevermore! *"And as Moses lifted up the serpent in the wilderness, even so must the Son of Man be lifted up, that whoever believes in Him should not perish but have eternal life"* (John 3:14-15).
Produces an old nature that makes every unsaved person a child of the devil. *"Ye are of your father the devil, and the lusts of your father ye will do"* (John 8:44a KJV).	Produces a divine nature. *"...that by these ye might be partakers of the divine nature, having escaped the corruption that is in the world through lust"* (2 Peter 1:4 KJV).

One of the things that you need to know is that each born-again person has two natures: the old nature from the old birth, and the new nature from the new birth. When we were born into our old nature, we were children of the devil. However, when we are born into the new nature through the new birth we become the children of God. That is why it is imperative that you receive the new birth. It is the only way to become a child of God.

Chapter Three

HOW CAN I BE BORN AGAIN? (PART TWO)

〜〜〜

Jesus answered, "Most assuredly, I say to you, unless one is born of water and the Spirit, he cannot enter the kingdom of God. That which is born of the flesh is flesh, and that which is born of the Spirit is spirit" (John 3:5-6).

In my mind, I can imagine Nicodemus inquiring of Jesus, "How can these things be?" No doubt, Jesus must have thought to Himself, "Wait a minute. This is Nicodemus. He is supposedly a master in Israel, and a learned man in the Laws of Moses, and he doesn't know the answer to these things?" Nicodemus had a stellar reputation of being a premier intellectual. He may have possibly served as the dean of the seminary in Jerusalem.

Had Nicodemus lived in our modern era, he might well have earned degrees and designations in the study of Rome and Israel. He understood and was able to explain governmental order at a moment's notice. He could dialog with the most politically astute men on governmental procedures of the republic. I am pretty certain that he would have been very emotional as he talked about the ill relationship between the patricians and the plebeians.

He would have talked about the struggle between these two social classes of people that lasted for more than 150 years. The patricians were a ruling class of politically driven people while the plebeians were descendants of former slaves. His opinion concerning the struggle would have been valuable since he was a learned man who had deep insight into the history of the Roman Empire.

A student of the Pentateuch (the first five books of the Law, or Bible), he was very knowledgable on Jewish history and the history of Israel, whose beginnings were found in its founding father, Abraham. In fact, it may have been the faith of Israel's founding fathers that further provoked his interest in a living and personal God. Even in the examples of the nation's forefathers, Nicodemus could clearly see a pattern of spirituality that mirrored the new birth. They had all known God in a very intimate way, and in their own personal ways, had experienced the new birth.

How Can I Be Born Again? (Part Two)

Abraham was born again when he stepped out in faith and left the land of his family. He journeyed to a new and strange country, looking for a city whose builder and maker was God. For him that was a new birth experience.

Moses was born again at the burning bush, when he took off his shoes and accepted the command to deliver the message to Pharaoh to let God's people go. This was his experience of a new birth.

David was remembered and revered for generations to come as a man after God's own heart. He experienced the new birth when he was in the prime of life, as the people were singing his praises, such as, *"Create in me a clean heart, O God; and renew a right spirit within me"* (Psalm 51:10 KJV).

Elisha was born again as Elijah's mantle was thrown upon his shoulders, empowering him to walk in the anointing of God.

> *So he departed from there, and found Elisha the son of Shaphat, who was plowing with twelve yoke of oxen before him, and he was with the twelfth. Then Elijah passed by him and threw his mantle on him* (1 Kings 19:19).

Jacob experienced the new birth when he wrestled with the angel of the Lord throughout the night, demanding God's blessing to be bestowed on him. He refused to release this angel until he received new life. As a result of his new birth, he received the new name,

Israel, to coincide with his matchless experience, replacing his old name and old deeds of the flesh.

Then Jacob was left alone; and a Man wrestled with him until the breaking of day (Genesis 32:24).

Nicodemus realized that each of these great men, ones whom he looked up to, had gone through the process of dying to become alive. Nicodemus, like them, would have to go through the same type of process, and so also do you.

For a moment, put yourself in Nicodemus' place. Nicodemus, I am going to give you a five-step crash program in Christian Education, which will start you off in the preschool years of spirituality and take you all the way through spiritual post-graduate studies. These five steps are the keys to understanding how one must be born again.

Before we get started on the steps, first rid yourself of what you already have. You ask, "What do you mean? Must I sell all of my belongings and give away my house and my car in order to be saved?" No, I'm not saying that at all. You have got to get rid of pride and prejudice. You must get rid of selfishness and self-righteousness, for those are all reflections of the old nature.

Jesus said it in this way:

Then He said to them all, "If anyone desires to come after Me, let him deny himself, and take up his cross daily, and follow Me" (Luke 9:23).

Each of us must deny himself. This is first done by giving up our old nature when we become new in Christ. The Apostle Paul said in 2 Corinthians 5:17, *"Therefore, if anyone is in Christ, he is a new creation; old things have passed away; behold, all things have become new."* By this standard, we must embrace what is new and abandon what is old for the sake of Christ and His Kingdom.

> *"Each of us must deny himself. This is first done by giving up the old nature."*

One of the major problems that I have identified in people who get saved is that many of them do not willingly abandon the old in order to make room for the new. They still desire to continue doing everything they practiced while they were in sin and try to force those practices to work in salvation. That is not how new birth works. In fact, if people choose not to abandon the old nature, eventually they will return to their old ways. I will talk more about that later in the next chapter.

Now let's examine those steps I was telling you about.

The First Step Is Faith. Faith is the foundation upon which Christianity is built. You cannot run this Christian race without faith. And even if it appears that you are able to get off to a fair start without faith, you will not be able to finish. For without faith it is impossible to please God. And it is only when you please God that He imparts supernatural strength to you for your journey.

If you exercise faith, then you have the answer. The answers that you need to win in life are hidden inside of your faith response toward God and His loving kindness. So for starters, you have to believe that by simply asking, God will save you. That's only the beginning. In time you will be able to walk by faith and not by sight in all matters.

"You cannot run the Christian race without faith."

But without faith it is impossible to please Him, for he who comes to God must believe that He is, and that He is a rewarder of those who diligently seek Him (Hebrews 11:6).

The Second Step Is Confession. I am sure that you may have heard the phrase *'fess up* before. It means that you need to make confession of the good, or not so good, deed that you did.

In the same manner, God fully expects His children to confess the good act of accepting the finished work of Jesus Christ. In order to be saved, you must confess the lordship of Jesus Christ. I've heard some people that claim to be shy say, "I really don't like speaking in front of people. I'd like to be saved, but I don't want to confess Jesus as Lord." There is a problem with that train of thinking. If you don't confess Him, then He will not confess you before His Father in heaven. Remember the roll call that your teacher took every morning when you were in grade school? The roll was taken to determine who was or was not in class that day. If you were in class, you responded aloud when your name was called. Much like this, Christ needs to hear your spoken confession to inform Him that you are in His presence. He needs to know that you are on His team.

> "When you confess Jesus as Lord, you are confessing your inability to save yourself."

When you confess Jesus as Lord of your life, you are confessing very powerful realities. One of the greatest realities is that you are confessing your inability to save yourself. You are showing the world that you are totally dependent on Jesus Christ for everything in life. *Everything* includes providing your finances, maintaining your health, having genuine friendships, providing for your food, shelter, and clothing, and maintaining mental and spiritual soundness.

Not to confess Jesus as Lord means that you still believe you can do something to save yourself or redeem yourself. That is arrogance, and God refutes pride and arrogance. You must first believe, then you must confess what you believe, and at that point you are already saved. However, there are a few more steps that you need to take to maintain the type of witness that will give God all of the glory.

For with the heart one believes unto righteousness, and with the mouth confession is made unto salvation (Romans 10:10).

49

The Third Step Is Patience. Don't be too hasty; take your time and wait on the Lord. The Bible says, *"The plans of the diligent lead surely to plenty, but those of everyone who is hasty, surely to poverty"* (Proverbs 21:5). The interesting thing about this scripture is that when the word *poverty* is mentioned it is not speaking only of financial poverty, but also of spiritual poverty.

There are so many people that receive Christ into their lives and want to be overnight spiritual giants. That is simply not reality. You cannot expect to be all that God intends for you to be and reach spiritual zeniths within days of your newfound commitment to the Lord. Growing in the things of God takes time. And, you've got to grow in grace every day. One songwriter once wrote, "We are climbing Jacob's ladder, every round goes higher and higher."

As you are going forward in the things of God, you may not always understand at first the long-term value. Just keep on climbing, keep working, keep hoping, and you will understand the mysteries of God better in time. Remember that patience and faith always work together. You cannot exercise biblical faith while omitting patience. Patience is the fuel that makes your faith become a reality. Remember that!

But those who wait on the LORD shall renew their strength; they shall mount up with wings like eagles, they shall run and not be weary, they shall walk and not faint (Isaiah 40:31).

How Can I Be Born Again? (Part Two)

I thank my God upon every remembrance of you, always in every prayer of mine making request for you all with joy, for your fellowship in the gospel from the first day until now, being confident of this very thing, that He who has begun a good work in you will complete it until the day of Jesus Christ (Philippians 1:3-6).

The Fourth Step Is Brotherly Kindness. The Bible tells us if we are to have friends, we must first show ourselves friendly. You must show kindness to those you meet. You must treat everybody right. This may sound a bit juvenile, but it is really important to your new birth experience. The ultimate reason that God saved you is really not about you, but rather about the people that He has called you to reach. God is very concerned about expanding His Kingdom. The only way that He will be able to do that is by having hosts of individuals who are concerned about God's concerns.

"When we show brotherly kindness toward others, we are demonstrating the character of God."

When we show brotherly kindness toward others, we are demonstrating the character of God. Not only that, we are also portraying an image of satisfaction concerning our salvation. The new birth makes the unfriendly friendlier. You will become so excited now that you have been made a brand-new person that it will show wherever you go.

Have you ever purchased a brand-new car, or maybe even a used car that felt brand-new to you? Maybe you know what it feels like to buy a new outfit, one that you have been wanting for a long time. The feeling you get when you wear that new outfit or drive that new car is such a phenomenal feeling that everyone who comes into contact with you feels your excitement.

Unfortunately, over time the car gets old. It may need to be repaired every now and then. Those outfits become outdated and in some cases obsolete. When that happens, your joy over owning those items diminishes. As a result, your expression toward people is not as friendly as it was when those things were brand-new, or even close to brand-new. The new birth should never be anything like that. God is always new, and salvation does not wear off. The joy related to your new birth should be as fervent today as it was when you were first born again.

One way that will become a reality is when you show an attitude of graciousness toward God's people. The attitude that says, "I'm saved, and I am loving it" will remain fresh and relevant as long as you continue to showcase your God like an attitude of friendliness. There really is no excuse for the born-again believer to be anything less than friendly to everyone. This is the way that God expands His Kingdom and draws people to Him.

The LORD has appeared of old to me, saying: "Yes, I have loved you with an everlasting love; therefore with lovingkindness I have drawn you" (Jeremiah 31:3).

The Final and Most Important Step Is Love. If we continue in the same framework of showing brotherly kindness, we come to the final step, the mother of all steps: love. Love is the growing part of our salvation. Love is an unqualified virtue. You don't love people because of who they are, what they can do for you, or for any particular reason. Rather, you love them in spite of everything. You have not genuinely received the new birth if you are hateful toward anyone. "Well," you ask me, "suppose someone intentionally tries to hurt me, use me, or do abusive things to me? Do I then have just grounds to withhold my love?"

When people do things against you that are totally abusive, harmful, scandalous, or just plain wrong, it is usually because they do not understand how to be loved. Most people in this category have never been properly loved. As a result, they cannot demonstrate proper love toward other people. We are ultimately the result of whom we have been mentored by throughout the course of our lives, whether consciously or unconsciously.

If you were unloved by your father, mother, or spouse, you will inevitably internalize the pain from such neglect, and then turn around and give the same poisonous bite to others within your circle. Love releases you from the pain of other people's wrongdoings. Love compels you to forgive your brother or sister. Jesus asked God, His Father, to forgive the people that crucified Him. Luke 23:34 declares, *"Then Jesus said, 'Father, forgive them, for they do not know what they do.' And they divided His garments and cast lots."*

Think about it. How could Jesus love these evildoers so much as to ask God to forgive them for their wrongdoing? It appears to me that they knew they were crucifying Jesus. But what they did not know was that they were crucifying the King of kings. Love is God, and God is love. Love validates *"Love releases* and authenticates your new birth in Christ. When you are *you from the* born again, you are born to love your brother and sister. *pain of other* When you were born into the *people's* flesh, you were born into sin, which made you susceptible to *wrongdoings."* hate, unforgiveness, and jealousy. Being born again delivers you from all of that through His love. *"Beloved, let us love one another, for love is of God; and everyone who loves is born of God and knows God. He who does not love does not know God, for God is love"* (1 John 4:7-8).

The Bible says that God loved me, not because I loved Him, but because He loved me first. It was not anything that I did that caused God to love me. *"For when we were still without strength, in due time Christ died for the ungodly. For scarcely for a righteous man will one die; yet perhaps for a good man someone would even dare to die. But God demonstrates His own love toward us, in that while we were still sinners, Christ died for us"* (Romans 5:6-8).

It does not matter how folks treat you—you still have to love them.

How Can I Be Born Again? (Part Two)

Now, Nicodemus, to complete this course you will have to be born of the water, of the blood, and of the Holy Ghost. In the same manner as natural water cleanses the body, the spiritual water will cleanse your soul, and before you know it, you will have *the right spirit!*

You'll soon partake in a commencement exercise in the School of Christ's Love. Before you know it, you will have a B.A. degree, which means you have been born again. After that, Christ Himself will confer upon you an M.A. degree, since you have been made anew. And simply by asking, you will receive the H.G. degree, being baptized with the Holy Ghost and fire.

Jesus said to Nicodemus, "I am not going to tell you when the day will come, but when it comes you will know it for yourself. When it comes, it will be like the wind. It blows where it wills. You can hear the sound of it, but you cannot tell where it came from or where it is going. Everyone who is born of the Spirit will have the same characteristics as the wind" (see John 3:5-8).

You cannot always tell when it is coming, but when it comes you will know it. Peculiar things will begin to happen in your soul. Something will get all over you. Jeremiah once lived through this great experience. He expressed it this way: *"Then I said, 'I will not make mention of Him, nor speak anymore in His name.' But His word was in my heart like a burning fire shut up in my bones; I was weary of holding it back, and I could not"* (Jeremiah 20:9).

When a Holy Ghost outpouring, which is a manifestation of the love of God, comes upon you, the little wheel will start turning. The fire of God will begin to burn inside of you. Rheumatic feet will start to run. Arthritic hands will begin to clap. Neither feet nor hands will sense any pain at all. If you have been born again, you will suddenly realize that you have the right Spirit. You won't be able to articulate exactly what happened to you. But you will know that it's all God.

The Role and Power of the Blood

And there are three that bear witness on earth: the Spirit, the water, and the blood; and these three agree as one (1 John 5:8).

For this is My blood of the new covenant, which is shed for many for the remission of sins (Matthew 26:28).

When I was a child we used to sing a wonderful hymn of the church entitled, "Nothing But the Blood of Jesus." The song opens posing the question, "What can wash away my sins?" Then the answers returns, "Nothing but the blood of Jesus." It continues, "Oh precious is the flow, that makes me white as snow, no other fount I know, nothing but the blood of Jesus." Each time that I would hear this song, I would be reminded that there was no other way to receive salvation than through the blood of Jesus.

You cannot receive salvation through efforts; nor can you receive salvation through intellectual skill. No matter how much money you have, you cannot purchase salvation for it is not for sale. It has already been paid for by a human's blood sacrifice—Jesus Christ. Salvation comes to those who understand just how the blood of Jesus washes away our sin. There is power in His blood. There is no other way to receive salvation than through Christ's shed blood. I cannot emphasize this point enough.

There are so many people that put unnecessary stress and weight on the shoulders of those seeking to have a relationship with Christ. Some have made others believe that their own efforts have something to do with their salvation. The only thing that you can do is to receive what has already been done. Any effort on your part to try to achieve or earn your salvation only disgraces Christ's sacrificial offering on the cross. Any attempts to earn or achieve salvation are tantamount to saying that what Jesus did on the cross was really not enough. They suggest that Jesus needs to go back on the cross, hang there for a longer amount of time, and lose gallons of blood.

> *"There is no other way to receive salvation than through Christ's shed blood."*

When He shed His blood on the cross, that sacrifice was more than enough to cover the high price of humanity's sin. Accept the fact that the blood did what you could never do for yourself. That is why I am so eternally grateful for the blood of Jesus. Without His blood, I would not be saved. I would not have a chance of succeeding at anything in life. His blood made my life not only worth living, but also highly valuable. His blood gave purpose and meaning to everything that I am, that I believe, and that I endeavor to live. The whole foundation of the Christian experience is totally connected and deeply entrenched in the blood of Jesus. His blood will make you brand-new.

Let's Review for Your Understanding

In order to receive your salvation, you must know these things.

1. Salvation is in your mouth—you will have what you confess.

2. You must believe. Your act of believing is what activates the power to produce the results of the words that you speak.

3. You need to have the right spirit. This means that your motive and heart need to be righteous. This does not mean that your spirit has to be pure before you can come to Jesus. If that were the case, you wouldn't need Him at all. What you need to have is an open mind and a humble spirit. That is the environment that Jesus wants to live within.

4. You must know for sure that there is power in the blood. It was the blood of Jesus that saved you, and without His blood you would still be charged with the high bill of sin, shame, and ultimate destruction. His blood covers your sin and washes you clean.

5. Because you are born again, everything about you should be different. As a truly born-again believer, you have experienced an entire overhaul. New believers' minds are different, their friends are different, and their worldview is totally different. After you are born again, you no longer enjoy the things that catered to your flesh. You now seek to please God in everything that you do.

Chapter Four

WHAT MUST I GIVE UP TO BE SAVED?

❦

So many people are scared to death to become believers because they are under the impression that in order to follow Jesus they will have to give everything up. I'm honored to say that they are right. But there is no need to be afraid. If you are going to follow Jesus wholeheartedly, you will have to relinquish any ties to this world or its debilitating influences. The really strange thing is that this spiritual mandate appears to be so peculiar at first. But if you really think about it, being asked to give up a material realm in exchange for peace, prosperity, and life forevermore, eternally abundant life should be the obvious choice.

Giving Everything Up

Let's look at this concept from the perspective of a couple potentially contemplating marriage. Even after engagement, some young men don't seem to really have a problem with keeping old phone numbers from their past relationships. They try to justify this by saying things like, "She is only a friend," and "I don't really think about her that way anymore." Whether those statements are true or false is not the point. The point is that if you are going to be married to someone and become totally faithful to that person, you will have to begin the right way.

The right way is by severing ties with anyone who held your attention in the past. You must learn to let things die. She could be the nicest person in the world. But your spouse-to-be now deserves undivided attention. And if she is wise, she will not begin her marriage sharing the stage with anyone from your past intimate relationships. Both you and I know that won't work. In a committed relationship, you are expected to leave behind the luggage from previous relationships.

This same train of thought can be clearly seen when looking at a person's citizenship to a certain country. Unless you are diplomat or a high-ranking governmental official sent to a nation for a particular purpose, you are not likely going to have dual citizenship in two countries. You are usually required to give up your citizenship in one country in order to embrace the values, governmental procedures, and overall system of another nation. There is really no real need to have dual citizenship. That is why it's not common to meet people who have dual citizenship.

Ultimately your loyalty will be toward the country that your heart is committed to. Hypothetically, let's suppose you had dual citizenship with the United States of America and Saudi Arabia. In the event that the United States of America went to war against Saudi Arabia or vice versa, who then would you defend? Whose side would you be on? Where would your loyalty stand? These are questions that you would definitely want to ask yourself before taking sides.

You would be in quite a quandary not knowing what to do. Why is that? It is simply because your loyalty will naturally have to fall on one side or the other. In the event that a crisis arises, you are going to gravitate toward the people, nation, or group that you believe in your heart you are willing to die for. You are probably not going to be willing to die for both countries, particularly if they are feuding for meaningless reasons.

Added to that, the country that you identify with can be seen in the expression of your cultural ways. Although America has long been a "melting pot," a place where people of varying backgrounds and ethnicities can live, grow, and prosper, it still has a distinguishable characteristic to everyone who dwells there. Most foreign-born people that have become Americans eventually adopt characteristics and a nature that are distinctly American. To be an American does not mean that you have to be born here, but rather, it means that you have embraced America's cultural ways.

That is why there are Italian-Americans, Irish-Americans, African-Americans, Polish-Americans, Jamericans (Jamaican-Americans), Latin Americans, Chinese-Americans, Russian-Americans, Israeli-Americans, and the list goes on and on. It's the same way in the body of Christ. No matter where you go in this world, you will always be able to identify others who belong to the body of Christ. No matter if they are from Europe, Africa, North America, South America, Asia, Central America, India, or even Antarctica, a fellow believer will be able to instantly identify them as part of the body. There is something different about them.

> *"When you are truly born again, you cannot love the ways of the world and God simultaneously."*

> *No one can serve two masters; for either he will hate the one and love the other, or else he will be loyal to the one and despise the other. You cannot serve God and mammon (Matthew 6:24).*

When you are truly born again, you cannot love the ways of the world and God simultaneously. You must choose to love and follow God above all. According to the scripture above, you will eventually come to hate one or the other. Either you will become a lover of the system of the world and hate God, or you will love the Lord and be in constant opposition with the world's system. You can't be on both sides.

What Must I Give Up to Be Saved?

Certain employers require you to sign a contract with them upon hiring you. Some companies require their employees to sign a contract that states that they are not allowed to work for another company in the same field while they employ them. There are some companies that will even take it a step further and prohibit a past employee from entering an agreement with a competing company within a certain amount of years after they have left the firm. Some restrictions may even prohibit the person from working within a certain distance of the last place. To some, this may sound pretty controlling. The real deal is that companies have to protect their investment, training, and privileged information from being misappropriated. My point is that you can't be loyal to two companies at once.

It's no different when you become born again. When you experience the new birth, the old things that you used to do will no longer be as appealing to you as they used to be. You have broken rank with those negative habits. You left them behind for something of far greater value. Now you are in an intimate relationship with the Lord and all of your past "cronies" are not invited.

I've heard people declare that they have left all to follow Christ. Some have left their families and friends to be wholly dedicated to the cause of Christ. Others have left addictive behavior behind in pursuit of God. Some have left financial empires behind to pursue His presence. The wonderful thing is that there is no one who has left behind any of these things for the sake of Christ and His Kingdom who hasn't received compensation in this lifetime for doing so.

No matter how hard it may seem at first, it always pays to give everything up for Jesus. It will pay not only in this lifetime, but also in the life to come. One sure thing is that Jesus Christ is the greatest example ever. What I mean by that statement is that He will never ask you to do anything that He has not first demonstrated by His own example. So when He asks us to leave everything behind in pursuit of Him, He has already proven that He first was willing to do so for our sakes.

Jesus never asks you to do anything that He has not first demonstrated by His own example.

Jesus Christ left the regal position that He held as a King to become like us. He was rich, but became poor for our sakes. What He left determined what came into His life. He left His imperial state only to be given a name that is above every other name. Just think about what you might receive if you are willing to part with the things that have been holding you back. You will never know how good life can be until you first give Jesus a try.

For you know the grace of our Lord Jesus Christ, that though He was rich, yet for your sakes He became poor, that you through His poverty might become rich (2 Corinthians 8:9).

So Jesus answered and said, "Assuredly, I say to you, there is no one who has left house or brothers or sisters or father or mother or wife or children or lands, for My sake and the gospel's, who shall not receive a hundredfold now in this time—houses and brothers and sisters and mothers and children and lands, with persecutions— and in the age to come, eternal life. But many who are first will be last, and the last first" (Mark 10:29-31).

Giving Up Bondage

One of the things that you must give up when you receive your salvation is bondage. Bondage is a category that contains many different subcategories. Whatever has kept you in bondage you need to surrender to Jesus. After you become saved, you are no longer a slave to sin, but rather a slave to Jesus. Whatever used to control you is now in your control.

On thinking about the word, you might think automatically about the obvious types of bondage. For example, some people are in bondage to sexual addiction, drugs and substance abuse, emotional and psychological disorders. These are what I call obvious bondages. There are, however, bondages that may not be as easily detected as the obvious ones, yet they are as equally oppressive as the obvious ones. Anything that seeks to control you is bondage. A person who has a controlling spirit over you is keeping you in bondage. When someone refuses to forgive himself, that person is putting himself behind prison bars.

"And you shall know the truth, and the truth shall make you free." They answered Him, "We

are Abraham's descendants, and have never been in bondage to anyone. How can you say, 'You will be made free'?" Jesus answered them, "Most assuredly, I say to you, whoever commits sin is a slave of sin. And a slave does not abide in the house forever, but a son abides forever. Therefore if the Son makes you free, you shall be free indeed" (John 8:32-36).

Jesus is truth. And once you get to know Him, you will be free. The more you know about Jesus, who is the Truth, the more He will shed light on your darkened situation. He literally will transform your entire life, freeing you from the clutches of evil. The Lord has freed some people who have gone back and entered into an agreement with the enemy, only to become enslaved all over again. They did not realize that their freedom was eternal. They did not realize that their freedom was conditional.

For you did not receive the spirit of bondage again to fear, but you received the Spirit of adoption by whom we cry out, "Abba, Father" (Romans 8:15).

When I speak of freedom being conditional, I am not suggesting that God is playing tit-for-tat games with His children. I am not suggesting that if you do one thing wrong, then everything that you have lived for will suddenly be destroyed—not that at all. What I am trying to convey is that you cannot have freedom unless you recognize the conditions in which freedom is actually realized. If someone has a driver's license, that person is completely free to drive that car anywhere he or she would like to go. That person is free to drive on public roads anywhere.

However, if that same person begins to speed, traveling 130 miles per hour in a 65-mile-per-hour zone, then he or she automatically and quickly will lose that freedom. That person will be arrested and put in jail. He or she had no respect and honor for that freedom. And whoever does not respect and honor their freedom will find themselves in bondage and being a slave to whatever is holding them back.

"You cannot look back at the things that you came out of as acceptable options in your new life."

But now after you have known God, or rather are known by God, how is it that you turn again to the weak and beggarly elements, to which you desire again to be in bondage? (Galatians 4:9)

After you become born again, why would you want to do anything that does not please God? Why would you want to partake in the things that are reminiscent of your unrighteous past? Those things directly correlate to your bondage. If God delivered you from crack addiction or cocaine use, you would be foolish to ever touch either substance again. For instance, you say

God saved you from alcoholism. Why then are you in the barroom every night after work? You used to be a chronic liar, and you still are. The only problem is that now you profess to be born again.

You cannot look back at the things that you came out of as acceptable options in your new life. When you get saved and are freed from the world's system and ways of doing things, you become separated into the purposes of God. Realizing that you have a higher purpose in life will humble you and give you the godly wisdom to make better choices about your actions and behaviors. You are called to serve God.

The Apostle Paul had a horrific life that included murder and regular persecution against God's people. Though it appeared that Paul was free to do whatever he wanted prior to his conversion, he was actually bound. After his conversion, he knew that he could never again look back into the bondage that had his mind thinking erroneously for so many years. He instantly became a bondservant of Jesus Christ, meaning that he was a slave to Christ. Romans 1:1 describes Paul as *"a bondservant of Jesus Christ, called to be an apostle, separated to the gospel of God."* He realized that the only true way to become free was to be bound to Him. Like Paul, you too must become bound to Christ in order to experience your freedom.

What Am I Gaining?

But now being made free from sin, and become servants to God, ye have your fruit unto holiness, and the end everlasting life. For the wages of sin is death; but the gift of God is eternal life through Jesus Christ our Lord (Romans 6:22, 23 KJV).

Some people wrongfully believe that when they get saved they are going to lose out on the finer things in life. They foolishly think that they will have to downsize their lives to mirror the poor of society. That is not true. The real truth is that once you get saved, you not only gain eternal life, but you also gain the Kingdom of God. The Apostle Paul clarifies exactly what the Kingdom of God is in his letter to the church at Galatia.

I say then: Walk in the Spirit, and you shall not fulfill the lust of the flesh. For the flesh lusts against the Spirit, and the Spirit against the flesh; and these are contrary to one another, so that you do not do the things that you wish. But if you are led by the Spirit, you are not under the law. Now the works of the flesh are evident, which are: adultery, fornication, uncleanness, lewdness, idolatry, sorcery, hatred, contentions, jealousies, outbursts of wrath, selfish ambitions, dissensions, heresies, envy, murders, drunkenness, revelries, and the like; of which I tell you beforehand, just as I also told you in time past, that those who practice such things will not inherit the kingdom of God. But the fruit of the Spirit is love, joy, peace, longsuffering, kindness, goodness, faithfulness, gentleness, self-control. Against such there is no law. And those who are Christ's have crucified the flesh with its passions and desires. If we live in the Spirit, let us also walk in the Spirit. Let us not become conceited, provoking one another, envying one another (Galatians 5:16-26).

When you possess the fruit of the Spirit, you possess the Kingdom of God. There is nothing greater than knowing that you have total peace and happiness in life. That is what most people are in search of. The Word of God lets us know that you already have this if you have Christ.

"When you possess the fruit of the Spirit, you possess the Kingdom of God."

Millions, perhaps billions, of dollars are spent annually on goods and services, nutritional supplements, dietary aids, self-help books, self-esteem seminars and workshops, motivational speakers, and prescription drugs all in search of wholeness. The sad thing is that after all of your money has been exhausted, often you will still find yourself in a position of lack, especially spiritual lack. There are some things in life that cannot be purchased. Salvation is one of those things. Also added to that all-star list are love, joy, peace, long-suffering, kindness, goodness, faithfulness, gentleness, and self-control. You cannot buy these things. However, God can birth them into your life by His Spirit.

We live in a world where gain is usually expected. Most folks don't like to do something and not receive anything in return for it. That is not inherently negative.

It is only common knowledge. If you put something in, then you expect to receive something from your investment. So when you invest your life in His, you become a recipient of the blessings of the Lord, or in other words, you receive His fruit. Your part is to offer your body to God as a seed. When you do that God will in turn give you the fruit of the Spirit that was born from that seed. Let's look at the fruit of the Spirit more definitively.

- Love—Agape, or God's unconditional love. You will be able to receive it and to give it.
- Joy—An unending cheerful spirit
- Peace—Total-life prosperity.
- Longsuffering—Patience.
- Kindness—Moral excellence in character; usefulness.
- Goodness—Moral purity.
- Faithfulness—Unwavering moral conviction. Total reliance on Christ.
- Gentleness—Total humility of spirit.
- Self-control—Temperance; never being indulgent in carnal passions.

Having all of these fruits planted into and continually growing inside you will cause your life to be so amazing that you'll have to question whether or not it's really happening. This is the good life that Jesus came to give to you. But beware! This is also the life that Satan continually seeks to steal from you, so you must be careful. You must be careful not to allow Satan to steal your joy or your peace and make you impatient. Don't allow him to defile your spirit, making you unclean. Resist any of his attempts to make you act totally out of control.

"Always remember that heaven is not abundant—it surpasses abundance."

When you give in to his schemes and deceptions, he will in turn steal everything that God has graciously given to you. So be careful to protect the gifts that God has given to you. *"The thief does not come except to steal, and to kill, and to destroy. I have come that they may have life, and that they may have it more abundantly"* (John 10:10).

Not only will you receive the fruit of the Spirit as a direct benefit of the born-again life, you will also receive abundant life. Always remember that heaven is not abundant—it surpasses abundance. You would be somewhat ill-informed to believe that the word *abundance* could actually be equated to God. God is bigger than abundance. *Abundance* is an English word attempting to describe a situation of having more than enough. God is beyond that. He is the One who keeps abundance supplied. So you must realize that abundance is an earthly word that can only be comprehended in an earthly sense. Jesus came to allow you to live in abundance on this earth. Not only did He die to give you abundance of the fruit of the Spirit, but He also died to give you an abundance of wealth and health.

What Must I Give Up to Be Saved?

Beloved, I pray that you may prosper in all things and be in health, just as your soul prospers (3 John 2).

God desires that you walk in divine health. He does not desire for you to be sick—ever. He does not want you to be unable to pay your bills. He does not want you to be in debt to creditors. Rather you should be the creditor extending credit to those who need it. Does God bless people with abundance just for the sake of having fine homes, fancy cars, and dream vacations? No, that is not the sole purpose why God blesses people with abundance. He blesses us to be a blessing to someone else.

He gives us an abundance so that we are able to minister to the needs of the poor and needy. God wants us to be so blessed that we are able to give to every good work. Just think about it for a moment. If you were financially well off, wouldn't you be a greater financial blessing to your church, foreign missions, evangelism ministries, your family, and medical organizations? Wouldn't you be able to help fund research to cure diseases, to help better educate our youth and children, and to build churches for Jesus? Of course you would. And because God knows that you will sow into areas that will ultimately extend His Kingdom, He continually brings financial increase opportunities to you. Remember that everything that you have given up for the sake of Christ's Kingdom will be given back to you in far greater measure. You will never lose with Jesus.

And God is able to make all grace abound to you, so that in all things at all times, having all that you need, you will abound in every good work. As it is written: "He has scattered abroad his gifts to the poor; his righteousness endures forever." Now he who supplies seed to the sower and bread for food will also supply and increase your store of seed and will enlarge the harvest of your righteousness. You will be made rich in every way so that you can be generous on every occasion, and through us your generosity will result in thanksgiving to God (2 Corinthians 9:8-11 NIV).

You Are Not Alone

One of the concerns that you sometimes feel when you make the step toward Jesus is that you are going to be all by yourself. The enemy does a strategic job of making you feel as if no one else is living a saved life but you. Believe me, at first it will appear to be that way. Most of the people that you used to deal with are probably not born again. And it will take some time for you to begin to recognize other people who are living the godly kind of life you are. Be encouraged! There are many people now and there were many people in prior times that perceived the benefits of leaving everything to follow Christ. They did it, and it worked for them. As you continue to move forward, you'll see it working for you also. If you don't believe me, here are some examples...

• Peter and the other disciples left homes and family.

What Must I Give Up to Be Saved?

Then Peter began to say to Him, "See, we have left all and followed You." So Jesus answered and said, "Assuredly, I say to you, there is no one who has left house or brothers or sisters or father or mother or wife or children or lands, for My sake and the gospel's, who shall not receive a hundredfold now in this time—houses and brothers and sisters and mothers and children and lands, with persecutions—and in the age to come, eternal life. But many who are first will be last, and the last first" (Mark 10:28-31).

• Abram, whose name would later change to Abraham, left his family and his country when he was a senior citizen.

Now the LORD had said to Abram: "Get out of your country, from your family and from your father's house, to a land that I will show you. I will make you a great nation; I will bless you and make your name great; and you shall be a blessing. I will bless those who bless you, and I will curse him who curses you; and in you all the families of the earth shall be blessed" (Genesis 12:1-3).

Abram left his entire family at an age when most men are looking forward to relaxing and spending quality time with their grandchildren. He knew by the Spirit that following God's voice would be greater in value than living in temporary comfort.

- Moses left the riches and grandeur of the Pharaoh's palatial kingdom to suffer with the people of God.

By faith Moses, when he became of age, refused to be called the son of Pharaoh's daughter, choosing rather to suffer affliction with the people of God than to enjoy the passing pleasures of sin, esteeming the reproach of Christ greater riches than the treasures in Egypt; for he looked to the reward (Hebrews 11:24-26).

- *All of the righteous are called to give up the comfort zone of not being criticized and condemned.*

Blessed are those who are persecuted for righteousness' sake, for theirs is the kingdom of heaven (Matthew 5:10).

For whoever desires to save his life will lose it, but whoever loses his life for My sake and the gospel's will save it. For what will it profit a man if he gains the whole world, and loses his own soul? Or what will a man give in exchange for his soul? For whoever is ashamed of Me and My words in this adulterous and sinful generation, of him the Son of Man also will be ashamed when He comes in the glory of His Father with the holy angels (Mark 8:35-38).

What Must I Give Up to Be Saved?

Now you need to write your own story. What have you left to follow Jesus? As an exercise, you can list those things in the following section. Just as in all of the biblical examples we discussed, God rewards each one for leaving family, businesses, status, fame, possessions, and a worldly mind-set. God will reward you, too. Since God gives the righteous men and women the desires of their hearts, it would be helpful to include also on your list the rewards you gained as a result. By seeing it in writing, you should clearly see that you have made the absolute, finest choice ever to follow Jesus.

Here is what I left behind:

_____

_____

_____

_____

_____

_____

_____

Here is what I gained:

_____

_____

_____

_____

_____

_____

_____

Chapter Five

SAVED BY GRACE

For by grace you have been saved through faith, and that not of yourselves; it is the gift of God, not of works, lest anyone should boast (Ephesians 2:8-9).

One thing that I want to leave with you is that there is nothing that you did to merit your salvation. Salvation did not come to you because your relatives are financially wealthy. You don't receive salvation because you are a star or because you play a leading role in a blockbuster movie. On the other hand, you don't automatically merit salvation just because you may have been born poor. God does not feel sorry for people and then save them on that account.

Perhaps you are a Rhodes scholar, or maybe you graduated magna cum laude from your college. That still does not qualify you to be saved. Regardless of whether you are a notable politician or a well-loved physician, those achievements will not earn you salvation. Salvation comes to a person one way and one way only—by grace. It comes by grace though the vehicle called faith. Not only will your life be unpleasing to God without faith, but also you literally can't be saved without exercising your faith.

"Grace is the bridge, or the connector, between God and man."

So, it is vitally important to exercise faith in every area of your life. It is also extremely important to understand God's grace. Now I realize that His grace is often so overwhelming that many people cannot comprehend it. I do not suggest that I fully comprehend His grace. All that I can give you is the revelation of His grace to me. And that is a small part. But I do believe that it is a sufficient part.

When people get saved, they do so by having faith in Jesus. Faith in any other name will not give you salvation. It must be the name of Jesus. So potential believers release their faith to God, and then God releases something back to those seekers called grace. Grace is the bridge, or the connector, between God and man. It is the way by which all blessing from God is transmitted. Without His grace, the flow of His blessings will stop immediately.

Think about the George Washington Bridge, the bridge that connects travelers to and from New York and New Jersey. If the bridge collapses and falls into the river, then travelers will have to find an alternate route to cross over. If that were to happen, millions of lives would be affected. It would literally slow the pace of production down for that entire region. United Parcel Service, Federal Express, and Airborne Express would all have to delay delivery of their packages to their clients. They would have to renegotiate the terms and agreements for their delivery practices. In some areas, they would have to cancel delivery all together. Why is this? The George Washington Bridge serves as a key connecting point to New York City. On the reverse side it serves as the avenue to Interstate 95, which connects many of the states along the East Coast. Without the bridge, that connection would be lost.

Now think about grace as your bridge to God. Without grace, love, happiness, and joy could not be delivered. Prosperity and healing would have to be put on hold because the bridge would be out. Worse yet, no one would be able to receive salvation, because without grace no one can be saved. The great news is that God's bridge of grace will not collapse. It has never been out of service or delayed. Anytime you need to receive anything from the Father, He sends it via His grace.

For the grace of God that brings salvation has appeared to all men, teaching us that, denying ungodliness and worldly lusts, we should live soberly, righteously, and godly in the present age, looking for the blessed hope and glorious appearing of our great God and Savior Jesus Christ, who gave Himself for us, that He might redeem us from every lawless deed and purify for Himself His own special people, zealous for good works (Titus 2:11-14).

Unlike any other religion of the world, Christianity stands alone in its distinctness as being a religion full of grace. The God that we serve is a very personal God, a very loving God, whose chief concern is to communicate His love toward us. He tries millions of methods to communicate His love toward us with expectations of us responding affirmatively to one or more of His ways.

What we all have to realize is that God is the builder of the bridge. He is the One who established the system for getting good things to us. We would be in grave danger to believe that we have done anything to afford such a privilege based on our own personal merits and strengths. There is nothing that we have done to establish the connection to God. This can only be credited to His nature and His goodness. There are many people who foolishly believe they can do something to earn salvation.

In grade school, I remember how the teacher used to give different kinds of awards for the children who behaved properly during class. Those who received the stickers, candies, or plastic toys were very proud to earn their rewards for behaving exceptionally. They had worked for it. You cannot work for salvation. It is a gift of God given by His grace alone. Any attempts to try to work for grace or earn grace will be futile.

Saved by Grace

But when the kindness and the love of God our Savior toward man appeared, not by works of righteousness which we have done, but according to His mercy He saved us, through the washing of regeneration and renewing of the Holy Spirit, whom He poured out on us abundantly through Jesus Christ our Savior, that having been justified by His grace we should become heirs according to the hope of eternal life (Titus 3:4-7).

There are many people that falsely believe they can merit their salvation by dressing a certain way or by performing a certain work or action. If that were truly possible, then eternal life would be reserved for the people that dressed well. Those who did not dress impeccably would not make it in. That's not how this thing works. I could not repeat this enough—salvation is by grace alone. The only part that you play in it is to willingly receive His grace.

But now the righteousness of God apart from the law is revealed, being witnessed by the Law and the Prophets, even the righteousness of God, through faith in Jesus Christ, to all and on all who believe. For there is no difference; for all have sinned and fall short of the glory of God, being justified freely by His grace through the redemption that is in Christ Jesus, whom God set forth as a propitiation by His blood, through faith, to demonstrate His righteousness, because in His forbearance God had passed over the sins that were previously committed, to demonstrate at the present time His righteousness, that He might be just and the justifier of the one who has faith in Jesus (Romans 3:21-26).

Therefore do not be ashamed of the testimony of our Lord, nor of me His prisoner, but share with me in the sufferings for the gospel according to the power of God, who has saved us and called us with a holy calling, not according to our works, but according to His own purpose and grace which was given to us in Christ Jesus before time began, but has now been revealed by the appearing of our Savior Jesus Christ, who has abolished death and brought life and immortality to light through the gospel (2 Timothy 1:8-10).

I'd like to take to take this opportunity to enlighten you on what grace actually is. Rather than dealing with what grace is not, which we will allude to later on, let's just look at what grace is. I've listed and commented on several facets of grace. I trust that this list will serve as a starting point for a better understanding of His grace. This is a starting point because your understanding will continually increase as you walk in the grace of our Lord. What you understood about grace last year might be far different from what you understood before that.

The Many Facets of God's Grace

Grace is the spring and source of all the benefits we receive from God. All of the blessings we receive can be attributed to His grace. God first saves us by His grace, and then He brings us into the place of living by His grace. We soon learn that He is our provider, not only of salvation, but also of all things. The Lord gives us grace, not only because He loves us, but also because grace is one of His personal, transcendent attributes. It's part of His nature, just like a good sense of humor or a strong work ethic may be part of your nature. It's simply part of who He is.

> *"Grace is the spring and source of all the benefits we receive from God."*

Better defined, grace is God's unmerited favor manifested toward both believers and unbelievers. Receiving God's grace is an indication that the demands of divine justice have been satisfied. Your penalty for sin was placed upon Christ and paid in full, making you eligible to receive the full benefits of being part of God's family. Through grace you are introduced into a new spiritual dimension—you are removed from death and moved into life. By grace we are fully and freely justified. Oh, what a glorious promise to claim!

Therefore, having been justified by faith, we have peace with God through our Lord Jesus Christ, through whom also we have access by faith into this grace in which we stand, and rejoice in hope of the glory of God (Romans 5:1-2).

Grace has many other facets as well. Grace is bestowed upon the righteous. It can restore us as well as save us. Grace comes to us through Christ alone. There is no other means of obtaining it. Christ's life was a platform on which grace was displayed. Through His death, grace for all mankind became possible. Grace is not only a gift, but also a living trust to keep!

Chapter Six

HOW TO FEED THE NEW MAN

〰〰

After you have been born again, the enemy will challenge you on every side. Quite truthfully, the enemy will try to do everything in his power to get you back. Every time he sees you worship and praise the Lord, he gets angry, realizing that he has lost one of his top recruits. You must be stronger than the enemy is. But you cannot do that by employing human wisdom and knowledge. The wisdom of God has to be your top priority in every area of your life from now on.

What I mean is that you must use God's Word as the basis for everything that you do. From the very simple choices in life to the foremost decisions that you make, God's Word must be your guiding light. Because of your need for grounding in God's Word, I have listed several very practical things that you can do on a regular basis.

Some of these practices will be on a daily basis and others several times each day. The objective is to get you so enamored with God and His Word that you literally will not have a second's worth of time to retrogress.

Reading the Word

Study to shew thyself approved unto God, a workman that needeth not to be ashamed, rightly dividing the word of truth (2 Timothy 2:15 KJV).

Although each subheading within this chapter is tremendously valuable to your spiritual nutrition, I believe that reading, studying, and meditating on God's Word is perhaps the greatest starting point for the new convert as well as the seasoned saint. We live in a generation where reading is really at an all-time low. Worse yet, men have the lowest reading levels, both in skill and time. In fact, women represent more than seventy-five percent of the entire book-buying market. The only subjects in which men may have a higher level of reading are the areas of business, computer technology, and automotive related journals. And yet, men still have marginal reading levels even in those categories. This information gives us some indication as to why our society is as spiritually deficient as it is. I believe that reading is fundamental to the growth and development of any culture. This means that reading God's Word is crucial for your growth as a Christian. Every single day, at least twice each day, you need to read God's Word.

How to Feed the New Man

Reading God's Word can be compared to the natural habit of eating food. Most people in the United States eat far too many foods with no nutritional value for the body. We may eat three to four times a day, but little of what we eat each day is healthy. Our culture has inundated us with a host of snack foods, junk foods, and fast foods that add to our girth but not to health. These types of foods leave us

"Reading God's Word is crucial for your growth as a Christian."

desiring more because our body's needs are not met. That is why many people in America are overweight and suffer from various kinds of sicknesses. Many of our illnesses are directly related to overeating or poor eating habits. Most people could not imagine missing a meal throughout the course of a day. Far more would consider suicide if they had to voluntarily go without eating for several days. I've heard people fuss and complain and even get into fights about food. When people are hungry, plain and simply, they want to eat.

Wouldn't it be wonderful if we displayed that same yearning for God's Word? Just as we need to feed our bodies nutritional foods to maintain good health, we also need to give our spirits the proper food to maintain good spiritual health. The food God gave us for our spirits is His Word. While books such as this are wonderful supplements for your spiritual diet, the main source of your spiritual nutrition is found only in the Bible. Your spirit man needs to be fed the Word of God, not once in a while, but daily.

This Book of the Law shall not depart from your mouth, but you shall meditate in it day and night, that you may observe to do according to all that is written in it. For then you will make your way prosperous, and then you will have good success (Joshua 1:8).

According to this scripture, your spiritual success in life directly correlates to having a balanced and complete diet of God's Word. You need to eat God's Word for breakfast. You must consume His Word for lunch. You must eat His Word for dinner. And when you feel hungry for a midnight snack, again you must eat His Word. In other words, the Bible must be a continual source of nutrition for your spirit man. If you feed on His Word continually, preferably at least two times each day, you will be more than likely to grow strong in your faith, not lacking in any area. In the same way that you prioritize healthy eating for your body, you must equally prioritize a diet of God's Word for a healthy spirit. By doing so, you will be strong and capable of defeating the enemy whenever he chooses to attack you.

Also, you must begin to eat daily portions of God's Word as soon as you receive Christ. There is an important reason behind this. Learning the fundamentals of your faith is foundational for your spiritual growth. When a person gets saved, he or she is likened to a newborn baby. Newborns need to be fed frequently in order to grow. The same is true of newborn believers. Without a constant source of nutrition, your spirit will weaken, leaving you susceptible to falling back into your old nature.

Not only do newborns need frequent feedings, but they also need a special diet. A physical newborn cannot eat a T-bone steak, macaroni and cheese, and a side of collard greens. They cannot eat food of that caliber even if it is strained. It's just too difficult for them to digest. They can only properly assimilate and digest mother's milk. Likewise, newborn believers also need a special diet. The Bible confirms this.

"Learning the fundamentals of your faith is foundational for your spiritual growth."

I fed you with milk and not with solid food; for until now you were not able to receive it, and even now you are still not able; for you are still carnal. For where there are envy, strife, and divisions among you, are you not carnal and behaving like mere men? For when one says, "I am of Paul," and another, "I am of Apollos," are you not carnal? (1 Corinthians 3:2-4)

For though by this time you ought to be teachers, you need someone to teach you again the first principles of the oracles of God; and you have come to need milk and not solid food. For everyone who partakes only of milk is unskilled in the word of righteousness, for he is a babe. But solid food belongs to those who are of full age, that is, those who by reason of use have their senses exercised to discern both good and evil (Hebrews 5:12-14).

"The milk of God's Word is the primary diet of a newborn believer."

The milk, or the basic principles, of God's Word is the primary diet of a newborn or young believer. A babe in Christ has different nutritional requirements from someone who is maturing in the faith. The newborn believer needs to establish a strong foundation in the basics of the Christian faith. Issues such as those found in this book should be established very soon in every new believer's life.

That doesn't mean that a mature believer does not need to feed on the milk any longer. Milk is beneficial for everyone. I was amazed to discover that a rising number of Olympians are purchasing natural breast milk from nursing mothers at a very high cost. Nutritionists say that mothers' breast milk contains all of the nutrients necessary for human growth and development. It's the perfect formula to maintain proper health, not only in babies, but also in adults. Some physicians and top trainers believe that by drinking mothers' breast milk and colostrum that Olympians will be able to perform optimally.

Whether you have been saved for one week or fifty years, it always benefits you to revisit the fundamentals of the Christian faith. Every now and again, you need to relearn the basics of the faith. Regardless of your level of maturity, you will never grow beyond the foundational truth of what your faith is built upon—the crucifixion, burial, and resurrection of Jesus Christ. Plain and simple, His blood was shed for the remission of your sin. And through that same blood, you have access to the Father's forgiveness and healing. Those things will always remain the same.

Yes, there are higher levels of maturity that you can attain in your Christian walk. Deeper issues that involve the Person and work of the Holy Spirit are food for more mature believers. But no matter how high you travel, you will always need the rudimentary lessons as your foundation. Those rudimentary lessons are the milk of the Word.

When people are first born again, they often want to know what parts of the Bible they should begin reading. I always suggest the book of Proverbs, for in it you will find words of wisdom by which to live. I also suggest that every new believer read all four Gospels (those are Matthew, Mark, Luke, and John) so that they can get a clear revelation of Jesus Christ. Then I believe that they should continue on in the Acts of the Apostles, so that they can understand that God is not just a god in theory but also One in power and demonstration.

A dislike for reading is not a reasonable excuse for avoiding Bible study. As a new believer, you cannot afford to neglect reading the Bible. It is your source for maintaining and growing in your faith. As you begin to read it and walk out its teachings, you will soon realize how the principles of His Word really work.

The law of the LORD is perfect, converting the soul; the testimony of the LORD is sure, making wise the simple; the statutes of the LORD are right, rejoicing the heart; the commandment of the LORD is pure, enlightening the eyes; the fear of the LORD is clean, enduring forever; the judgments of the LORD are true and righteous altogether. More to be desired are they than gold, yea, than much fine gold; sweeter also than honey and the honeycomb (Psalm 19:7-10).

Attending Bible Teaching

How then shall they call on Him in whom they have not believed? And how shall they believe in Him of whom they have not heard? And how shall they hear without a preacher? (Romans 10:14)

We live in an age where going to church has become so diminished that people use every possible excuse to justify not going at all. Worse yet, they don't feel the slightest remorse. For them, it's okay not to attend church. In fact, many people will tell the preacher or parishioner, "It doesn't matter whether or not I go to church. I read my Bible and pray every day." Some people have the gall to admit, "I'm too busy to go to church on Sundays." Or, "My kids have basketball, football, or soccer games to attend." Or, they'll say, "I have to do my laundry or catch the latest movie."

Whatever your excuse might be, I want you to know for the record that it's not acceptable to avoid going to church. You might say, "Well, pastor, I've been hurt by the church before." Suppose that you were hurt by a lawyer before, yet you suddenly find yourself in need of legal counsel. Would you refuse to employ the services of a lawyer because you've been hurt before? Of course not! You can't hold all lawyers responsible for the actions of one, so why would you hold all churches responsible for the actions of one church? When it comes to the church, why make unnecessary excuses for not attending God's house? Don't be deceived by the devil or by society. The truth is that you cannot grow spiritually if you are not hearing God's Word often.

"It's not acceptable to avoid going to church."

Some people falsely believe that they can teach themselves the Word of God and that they don't really need the preacher. But that is not what God's Word says. You cannot hear without a preacher. Now, I'm not saying that no one other than the preacher hears from God. That's not what I'm trying to get across to you. What I'm trying to convey is that there is a special word from God that is vital to your sustenance that only comes from the preacher. God has placed an anointed word in the mouth of your man or woman of God just for you. Once you hear that word, burdens will be removed and yokes will be destroyed off your life forever. However, it is your responsibility to be at the right place at the right time to hear the word from God—and that place is at your church.

Over the years, I can remember times when I preached a life-changing word to the congregation. I would witness many people being set free from the powers that held them back far too long. The people, who I knew in my spirit should have been there, were not. I'm talking about the people who were struggling in the area on which I was preaching; they would not show up for service that night. As a result, they did not receive their deliverance.

They would come up to me the next time they decided to come to church, and they'd say, "Apostle, I am really struggling with a particular issue. I don't know what to do, and I would really appreciate it if you would pray for me right now." Believe me when I tell you that I really do not have any problems with praying for people. It is my joy and pleasure to do so. However, right after I've finished preaching a message and am on my way back to my office is not the most appropriate time to flag me down for a prayer meeting. I've already poured out of my spirit all that God has given me for that morning. My desire at that moment is to be able to sit down and begin to regroup, so that I can receive spiritual and natural replenishing. The first thought that comes to mind is, "Why wasn't this person here for the past seven or eight Bible studies? Why wasn't he here the past Sunday? If he had only been here, he would have received what everyone else received."

Some people tend to think that twice or three times per week is too much time to spend in church. If you are under that impression, I have a question for you. How many times in the past year or so has the devil been on strike? How many times has he taken a vacation or even gone on a sabbatical? You already know the answer. Satan never takes time off, which means that he is relentless in his efforts to destroy your life. He gets more wicked every day as time continues on. His diabolical tactics become increasingly more fiendish. The attacks that he launches become more deadly.

"Satan never takes time off from his efforts to destroy your life."

That should send a signal to you that you need to be on guard at all times. How can you know how to defend yourself from him when you're living in isolation from the body and when you don't know the Word?

Every time you go to church, not only do you have the distinct pleasure of praising and worshipping God, but you also get informed on how to defeat the enemy in every area of your life. So you think you've heard so many messages and have been taught so well that you no longer need to hear God's Word? Wrong! Satan is learning more sophisticated tactics. If the last ones he used didn't work, he will go back into his workshop to figure out new ones that will. You must make it your job to be as diligent in your defense as he is in his attacks. He won't stop and neither should you.

Each time you come to Bible teaching and Sunday morning worship, God imparts a supernatural strength into your soul. The more you continue to come, the stronger you will become, and soon the enemy will not know what to do with you. He will be forced to target someone who is far more vulnerable than you are. Don't miss out on the privilege to receive teaching and instruction as often as possible. Each and every word from God will literally make you stronger. Remember that the preacher (those who operate in the fivefold ministries of apostle, prophet, evangelist, pastor, and teacher) was given to you by God for your betterment. The more you hear the better you will become.

But to each one of us grace was given according to the measure of Christ's gift. Therefore He says: "When He ascended on high, He led captivity captive, and gave gifts to men." (Now this, "He ascended"—what does it mean but that He also first descended into the lower parts of the earth? He who descended is also the One who ascended far above all the heavens, that He might fill all things.) And He Himself gave some to be apostles, some prophets, some evangelists, and some pastors and teachers, for the equipping of the saints for the work of ministry, for the edifying of the body of Christ, till we all come to the unity of the faith and of the knowledge of the Son of God, to a perfect man, to the measure of the stature of the fullness of Christ; that we should no longer be children, tossed to and fro and carried about with every wind of doctrine, by the trickery of men, in the cunning craftiness of deceitful plotting, but, speaking the truth in love, may grow up in all things into Him who is the head—Christ—from whom the whole body, joined and knit together by what every joint supplies, according to the effective working by which every part does its share, causes growth of the body for the edifying of itself in love (Ephesians 4:7-16).

Listening to Preaching and Teaching Tapes

So then faith comes by hearing, and hearing by the word of God (Romans 10:17).

If you don't hear teachings over and over again, you will eventually lose them. Most everything that you hear isn't retained unless you hear it consistently. That's why you need to hear solid Bible teachings more than once. It's absolutely amazing how you will gain a deeper understanding of God's Word each time that you hear it. It could be the same teaching, yet the Holy Spirit will reveal another facet of that message to you each time you hear it.

Getting teaching tapes of the service is a good way to keep up with the preacher's teachings when you can't be present during church services. Nowadays, most churches make this option available. Even when you *are* in a service, getting the tapes can be beneficial. There are always distractions that may keep you from receiving what is being taught. The enemy comes to church too, you know. Sometimes the distraction can be as simple as your child running around or talking while the sermon is going on. No matter how anointed the message is, distractions can keep you from fully enjoying the message or gaining instruction from it.

Having the tapes lets you catch what you've missed. And it can be a blessing to re-listen to a message and meditate on it during your private quite time with the Lord. You will never develop faith for anything if you only hear a truth once. Hearing something one time may not convince you of its reality. When you hear the same thing repeatedly, it becomes real to you.

> *"You will never develop faith for anything if you only hear a truth once."*

Listen to teaching tapes and CDs in your car, in your home, or anywhere you are. Every opportunity that you can get to reinforce what you have already heard will help you to become more knowledgable. Just as a flower grows up healthy with proper care, so will your spiritual maturity develop as you seize every opportunity to feed your spirit with God's Word.

Watching Video Recordings

Although our spiritual walk is predicated on faith and not sight, some people really need to see visuals in order to strengthen their faith. People by nature are visually oriented. You may have heard the phrase: "One picture speaks a thousand words." That phrase is really true. Pictures help many people to understand things better. When a child first starts attending school, the teacher always uses colorful paintings and illustrations to get the child interested in learning how to read.

It's the same way with spiritual children. In the beginning, visuals help new converts to recognize the godly truths being articulated in the message. However, the benefits of visuals are not limited to small children. We are a visually oriented culture. Most of us adults thoroughly enjoy reading our favorite magazines when they are loaded with colorful, real-life pictures. It makes the magazine more exciting and enjoyable. Some of us may grow beyond needing a visual experience in order to comprehend a sermon or message; however, others may continue to learn best that way. Each of us must discover the ways that we most effectively learn. From my experience and observation, I have seen many people benefit and grow through the use of teaching videos, not only at our church, but also at other ministries.

Remember that Jesus Christ Himself used visuals and picture images when He told parables. He knew the tremendous power of being able to get people to see the bigger picture. If God gets the glory, and people are continually becoming better disciples, then let's encourage people to use, support, and promote the sales of Christian audio and visual materials.

Having Small Group Bible Study with Your Family

Train up a child in the way he should go, and when he is old he will not depart from it (Proverbs 22:6).

Parents are responsible for teaching and training their children in the ways of the Lord. Our society has become so perverted and unrighteous because so many people have not understood the value of the principle set forth in Proverbs 22:6. If you train your children in the way that they should go, when those children become adults, they will be more inclined to adhere to what you taught them.

"Parents are responsible for teaching and training their children in the ways of the Lord."

Unfortunately, in our society children are as equally involved in negative things, such as promiscuity, theft, rape, selling drugs, drug addiction, illegal gambling, gang involvement, and even murder as adults are. In many cases, their connection to these crimes go far beyond the involvement of adults. This should not be. The reason why this happens and is continuing to happen at alarming rates is simply because children are no longer being trained.

When I was a child in South Carolina, most children knew well that all the adults within our community had unspoken permission to help raise everyone else's children. If any of us children did something mischievous, we would be reprimanded by an adult who had witnessed what we did. We would not dare tell our mother or father that we got in trouble and Mr. or Mrs. "So 'n' So" had to discipline us. We knew when that happened we would be in for a grand whipping from our parents.

Our parents expected us to behave as exemplary children, particularly in public. We could not act out, or misbehave, or do things that were totally ridiculous, because they had taught us how to behave properly. I said they "taught us" the difference between how we should behave and how we should not. They gave us structure, something that is grossly lacking in our society today. We knew that we were not going to do just anything we wanted when we were not in the presence of our parents, because we had conviction within us reminding us of what we were taught.

It is so important as a parent, an aunt, or an uncle to train children in the ways of the Lord. Teach them the Holy Scriptures. Show them, by example, the value and benefit of living a holy life. When you teach your family the Word of God, three major things happen that are directly connected to your personal walk with God. The first thing that happens is that you will develop a strong appreciation for God's Word each time you teach it to your family.

Secondly, you will become better at living God's Word because you teach it. It is said that the best way to master something is to teach it. When you teach it, you become good at it. It is one thing to keep hearing God's Word over and over, but when you begin to teach what you've learned, then you become skilled at living out its principles, especially because you have become responsible for helping others to learn them.

Thirdly, you will become accountable to the people that you teach. Your family will keep you on your "p's" and "q's." They'll expect you to model what you have taught them. Whatever you teach, you become accountable for the words taught. If you teach you children not to quarrel and fuss with one another, then they will not tolerate it if you should begin fussing and arguing with your spouse. If you teach a child not to steal, then you should never have the slightest temptation to do so. If you teach your family to love one another and love all people because God made them, then they should never hear you speaking prejudicial words about anyone.

There is a saying that goes like this: "What you see is what you get." I could take that one step further by saying, "What you teach is what you get." If our community is to change for the better, we have to start teaching our young people what God's Word says. Stop depending on the preacher to do everything. The preacher's job is to reinforce what you are teaching in your home. His or her efforts become useless if you are not teaching the same things in the home. Teaching will not only help to strengthen those around you in the things of the Lord, but it will also strengthen you in the process.

Having Small Group Bible Study with Your Fellow Employees

So continuing daily with one accord in the temple, and breaking bread from house to house, they ate their food with gladness and simplicity of heart, praising God and having favor with all the people. And the Lord added to the church daily those who were being saved (Acts 2:46-47).

One way to grow spiritually is to share what you have been taught with your fellow employees.

Establish a Bible study at your job among believers of like faith. It's a sad thing when you proclaim to be Christian yet your coworkers don't know that you are saved. Your salvation should not be a big secret. It should be known to all of your friends, family, and coworkers.

"Invite your non-believing coworkers to a Bible study."

I've heard believers complain about how the people at their jobs are just so ungodly. They'll say, "These people swear, cuss, fuss, and talk a whole lot of ungodly talk all day long." "When I get home from work, I just feel so dirty and unclean." How can you change that? You will never change your environment by simply talking about how bad it is. The proactive thing to do is to start a Bible teaching once or twice each week at your job. Start it with other people of like precious faith. Then begin to invite your non-believing coworkers to the study. Believe me, you will notice that the overall atmosphere at your job will become far more peaceful. God's Word will literally infuse the atmosphere with His glory. More than that, you will not allow the enemy to take over your workplace, but rather you will be taking over his territory and consecrating it for the purposes of the King.

Praying and Communing with God Daily

In the same manner He also took the cup after supper, saying, "This cup is the new covenant in My blood. This do, as often as you drink it, in remembrance of Me." For as often as you eat this bread and drink this cup, you proclaim the Lord's death till He comes (1 Corinthians 11:25-26).

Communion is more than just a sacred rite involving the bread and the wine. Communion is a lifestyle for the Christian. We commune and communicate with God every single day. Prayer is a type of holy communion with God. I cannot stress enough, for both new convert and seasoned saint, that you must talk to the Lord in prayer every day.

"Prayer is the lifeline between you and the Lord."

In fact, you should pray often throughout each day. Prayer is the lifeline between you and the Lord. It's what keeps all of your spiritual vital organs functioning well. If you decrease the consistency of your prayer life, your walk with God will begin to break down slowly. It may not be visible at the very beginning, but it will definitely show over time. Prayer is what keeps the enemy away. Prayer literally torments the devil. Every time we pray we are sharing intimate conversation with Jesus.

Not only should we never neglect to pray, but we should also never neglect to participate in the rite of Holy Communion with other believers. You must remember that significance of the bread in Holy Communion has to do with the broken body of our Lord. When we choose not to unite with other believers, then we are dividing His body that much more. We become united as one body through partaking in this Holy Sacrament.

How to Feed the New Man

From early on, every believer needs to study, understand, and faithfully practice praying and participate in Holy Communion. In the same way that proper health, dieting, and relaxation all help to extend life, these practices will help to support your spiritual development throughout your entire walk with Jesus. Just as bad habits are hard to break, good habits are difficult to break also. Make praying and communing with God daily habits in your life that you refuse to break. The benefits will be beyond your imagination.

Taking Notes

Then the LORD answered me and said: "Write the vision and make it plain on tablets, that he may run who reads it" (Habakkuk 2:2).

Write down every important thing your minister says. Keep a spiritual journal of all the progress you are steadily making. You'll be amazed at just how much you have developed spiritually over a period of time. It's good to write down things so that your level of retention of what you've learned will increase. Another reason why you should write things down is because you become accountable to that which you put in writing. It's difficult to deny that you've learned something when the evidence of it exists in your own handwriting.

Finally, you should write things down as an encouragement to yourself. Writing things down charts your progress. It lets you know where you were, spiritually speaking, one or two years ago. It lets you see how you took many small steps to get to where you are now. You won't become a giant in the faith over night, and that is completely all right. The point is to strive to make measurable progress each day. Start on the milk of the Word, and then move on to the meat. Your healthy growth awaits!

> *Therefore, laying aside all malice, all deceit, hypocrisy, envy, and all evil speaking, as new-born babes, desire the pure milk of the word, that you may grow thereby, if indeed you have tasted that the Lord is gracious* (1 Peter 2:1-3).

Chapter Seven

WHAT IF I FAIL?

~~~~~~~~~~

If the disciples had never failed, they never would have gathered the great lesson to be learned from having faith in an unfailing God. Success is only birthed in failures. Many others look upon my church and me today and automatically believe that I am a successful man with a successful ministry. That is true; however, both my church and me have experienced failures over the years. We refused to allow those failures to become our end or to threaten our vision.

Learning the Secret of Getting Up Again

As a church, we sometimes failed, and at times I myself sometimes failed, but we did not stay in that place of failure. I immediately began to seek God in the midst of failure, asking Him to reveal the master plan on how I could get out of whatever predicament I found myself in. So truthfully, I can't say that I wish I never failed in life. I personally believe that would be a most immature statement. If I had never failed, then I never would have learned how to overcome it. So, in some ways, one can look at failure as an opportunity to become educated in the school of the Holy Spirit.

"Success is only birthed in failures."

In the school of the Holy Spirit, the Lord ministered to me in some very interesting ways that I believe will help any believer to spring back from life's failures. Far too many people stay in a defeated position. Too many people feel totally controlled by exterior forces. What they don't realize is that God has given you the power to control how you react to things in life. And usually, it is in our reactions that we ultimately determine whether or not we will succeed. Here are some things that I learned:

Learn how to control your reaction to your circumstances. You cannot always control your circumstances in life, because things are often beyond your power. Just because things are beyond your control does not mean that you have to behave uncontrollably. Your reaction often determines how long you will have to deal with your problem. Remember, in some situations it is better not to respond at all.

Use your bad circumstances as a stepping stone to your success. Sometimes you can use negativity to fuel your tank. There have been times in my life when people with preconceived notions about me have told me that I wouldn't make it. Their words only made me that much more eager to live beyond their assumptions. If they said that I couldn't do it, then I was determined to prove to them that I could do all things through Christ. I've learned that as long as I have Jesus I cannot fail.

Focus on Jesus

Immediately Jesus made His disciples get into the boat and go before Him to the other side, while He sent the multitudes away. And when He had sent the multitudes away, He went up on the mountain by Himself to pray. Now when evening came, He was alone there. But the boat was now in the middle of the sea, tossed by the waves, for the wind was contrary. Now in the fourth watch of the night Jesus went to them, walking on the sea. And when the disciples saw Him walking on the sea, they were troubled, saying, "It is a ghost!" And they cried out for fear. But immediately Jesus spoke to them, saying, "Be of good cheer! It is I; do not be afraid." And Peter answered Him and said, "Lord, if it is You, command me to come to You on the water." So He said, "Come." And when Peter had come down out of the boat, he walked on the water to go to Jesus. But when he saw that the wind was boisterous, he was afraid; and beginning to sink he cried out, saying, "Lord, save me!" And immediately Jesus stretched out His hand and caught him, and said to him, "O you of little faith, why did you doubt?" (Matthew 14:22-31)

I've heard a lot of preachers sharply criticize Peter as being a person who had little faith. They've condemned Peter harshly, telling their audiences that Peter took his eyes off of Jesus and began to sink. They exposed Peter's fears and inner inhibitions about life. If they were to be totally honest, they would have to admit that they, too, have taken their eyes off of Jesus. We all have from time to time.

All of us have times when we go through situations that cause us to doubt and fear. We're concerned because we don't know how our situation will turn out. While in the midst of it, we feel frightened. But we're in good company because few believers are exempt from times like these.

I realize that there are whole groups of church people that don't want to admit they have feelings and emotions. They want everyone else to believe that they go through life without any moments of feeling uncertain. Well, God bless them, if this is true for them. I, for one, have moments in my life when I'm not as clear as I would like to be on certain matters. And there have been times in my walk with the Lord that my eyes were not as fastened on Jesus as they should have been. Where did that place me? Was I a wretched soul for having been in a place of uncertainty? Should I have gone to hell for taking my eyes off of Jesus and being distracted by the cares of this world? I think not. One of the things you need to learn about Peter and his walk on the water is that he did not totally take his eyes off of Jesus. Had he totally taken his eyes off of Jesus, he would have perished the moment he set foot in the water. And another thing, those doubtless believers always fail to mention that there were eleven other disciples who never had the courage to get out of the boat. Perhaps you experience the situations you do because you willingly stepped into the water.

Have you ever driven down the road and seen an accident and stared at it so intently while driving by that you almost got into an accident yourself? If you stayed focused on that accident, you, too, would have crashed. But in a split second, your mind reminded you of your need to focus on the road ahead in order to ensure your safety. That's how Peter responded. Yes, he took his eyes off of Jesus, but he set his focus in the proper place once again to avoid his demise.

Okay, so maybe you have gotten off focus for too long now. God is trying to convey a simple message to you: Refocus. Get you eyes back on Jesus and everything will realign itself again. If you're caught in the dark, then you must seek out the light, Jesus Christ. Don't quit. Don't get discouraged. Don't give up. Refocus your attention on the Giver of light, and you will find yourself once again where you belong.

This is the message which we have heard from Him and declare to you, that God is light and in Him is no darkness at all. If we say that we have fellowship with Him, and walk in darkness, we lie and do not practice the truth. But if we walk in the light as He is in the light, we have fellowship with one another, and the blood of Jesus Christ His Son cleanses us from all sin. If we say that we have no sin, we deceive ourselves, and the truth is not in us. If we confess our sins, He is faithful and just to forgive us our sins and to cleanse us from all unrighteousness. If we say that we have not sinned, we make Him a liar, and His word is not in us (1 John 1:5-10).

Don't Quit!

I want you know that if you have ever failed or fallen short in life you are not alone. Many of the greatest leaders in the Bible have at one time failed. Yet they did not stay there. I've listed below several scriptures that do not promote failure, but rather offer a godly alternative to failure. Jesus is that alternative. You do not have to be a failure in life. You ask, "What makes me a failure?" The only thing that will make you a failure is if you willingly choose to quit.

"The only thing that makes you a failure is if you willingly choose to quit."

When you quit, it is an affront to the Kingdom of God. It is a slap in God's face. Because when you quit, you are simply telling God that you don't believe He has the power to give you the victory in your next round. You may have lost many rounds in life. Things may look increasingly negative. Maybe it seems like there is no hope for you. Those are the kinds of situations that God truly desires to work in.

When everything looks bleak, when it seems like all hope is lost, that is when God steps in to give you the victory. But He can only do that for a person who is willing to fight until the victory has been won. So what if you have fallen. Get back up and let God fight for you. It will appear as if you are doing the fighting, but you know that God is really the One throwing all the punches.

Here is a list of scriptures that will encourage you as you continue to fight on toward your victory.

Confess your trespasses to one another, and pray for one another, that you may be healed. The effective, fervent prayer of a righteous man avails much (James 5:16).

For a righteous man may fall seven times and rise again, but the wicked shall fall by calamity (Proverbs 24:16).

He shall deliver you in six troubles, yes, in seven no evil shall touch you (Job 5:19).

Many are the afflictions of the righteous, but the LORD delivers him out of them all (Psalm 34:19).

Though he fall, he shall not be utterly cast down; for the LORD upholds him with His hand (Psalm 37:24).

Do not rejoice over me, my enemy; when I fall, I will arise; when I sit in darkness, the LORD will be a light to me. I will bear the indignation of the LORD, because I have sinned against Him, until He pleads my case and executes justice for me. He will bring me forth to the light; I will see His righteousness. Then she who is my enemy will see, and shame will cover her who said to me, "Where is the LORD your God?" My eyes will see her; now she will be trampled down like mud in the streets (Micah 7:8-10).

We are hard pressed on every side, yet not crushed; we are perplexed, but not in despair; persecuted, but not forsaken; struck down, but not destroyed—always carrying about in the body the dying of the Lord Jesus, that the life of Jesus also may be manifested in our body. For we who live are always delivered to death for Jesus' sake, that the life of Jesus also may be manifested in our mortal flesh. So then death is working in us, but life in you (2 Corinthians 4:8-12).

Are they ministers of Christ?—I speak as a fool— I am more: in labors more abundant, in stripes above measure, in prisons more frequently, in deaths often. From the Jews five times I received forty stripes minus one. Three times I was beaten with rods; once I was stoned; three times I was shipwrecked; a night and a day I have been in the deep; in journeys often, in perils of waters, in perils of robbers, in perils of my own country-men, in perils of the Gentiles, in perils in the city, in perils in the wilderness, in perils in the sea, in perils among false brethren; in weariness and toil, in sleeplessness often, in hunger and thirst, in fastings often, in cold and nakedness—besides the other things, what comes upon me daily: my deep concern for all the churches. Who is weak, and I am not weak? Who is made to stumble, and I do not burn with indignation? If I must boast, I will boast in the things which concern my infirmity. The God and Father of our Lord Jesus Christ, who is blessed forever, knows that I am not lying (2 Corinthians 11:23-31).

Chapter Eight

ETERNALLY SECURE

❧❧

It's important that you know, without any doubts, that you are totally and completely saved no matter what anyone says to you. You must understand and be assured that your salvation is secured for eternity. There are people who teach doctrines that are extremes on both sides of this issue—extremes that are not biblical. One extreme is the belief that once you get saved anything you do that is remotely wrong will cause you to lose your salvation and sentence you to eternal fire and damnation. Those who believe this extreme teach that if you make a mistake you are headed for hell. They falsely believe that once you get saved you will never have any temptations or failures. The real truth is that after you have confessed salvation the enemy will try even harder to get you to do things that are dishonoring to God.

The other extreme is the belief that you can live any way you choose and God will just have to tolerate your foolishness. That is as equally as untrue as the other extreme. There are things that you can do to lose your salvation. If there were not, then the term *reprobate* would not even exist.

"You must understand and be assured that your salvation is secured for eternity."

And even as they did not like to retain God in their knowledge, God gave them over to a **reprobate** *mind, to do those things which are not convenient; being filled with all unrighteousness, fornication, wickedness, covetousness, maliciousness; full of envy, murder, debate, deceit, malignity; whisperers, backbiters, haters of God, despiteful, proud, boasters, inventors of evil things, disobedient to parents, without understanding, covenant breakers, without natural affection, implacable, unmerciful: who knowing the judgment of God, that they which commit such things are worthy of death, not only do the same, but have pleasure in them that do them* (Romans 1:28-32 KJV, emphasis mine).

Ever learning, and never able to come to the knowledge of the truth. Now as Jannes and Jambres withstood Moses, so do these also resist the truth: men of corrupt minds, **reprobate** *concerning the faith* (2 Timothy 3:7-8 KJV, emphasis mine).

A *reprobate* is one who continues to reject God. If you have been truly born again, you don't have to worry about the chances of being a reprobate. Your salvation is secure. What makes me so sure? I know beyond any doubt that Jesus' shed blood on the cross gave me access to eternal life simply by asking for it. If I do not ask, then I cannot receive. However, if I ask, I can be completely assured that God will grant me an irrevocable salvation. What I mean by that is that no one can take away my salvation. Added to that I cannot lose my salvation simply because I made a mistake.

God is not vindictive like so many of us are. Could you imagine how life would be if you or your friends were God for a day? All of your enemies and the people that did immoral things or unfair things against you would be immediately sentenced to hell without question or a fair trial. Humans have such a propensity to be harshly evil toward each other that it is really saddening.

Even pastors at times can be so unloving and unforgiving. One of the things that I have never forgotten since Jesus called me to the ministry is that His is a ministry of love and reconciliation. Also, I have never forgotten that we are in the business of winning souls to the Lord. After listening to some pastors preach, you'd be inclined to believe that they are in a partnership with the devil trying to recruit people to go to hell. If a preacher preaches about hell with greater conviction than he preaches about heaven, then something is grossly wrong with that picture.

I've had groups of people get angry with me when I teach that the believer (not the sinner) has eternal security. From their perspective, they would have us believe that God has us on His big game board, just waiting for the opportunity to cast us off if we fail Him.

That may be the picture some folks have of God, but that's not the God we read about in the Bible. God is the most patient, longsuffering, and loving God that you will ever know. You ask, "Well, what about His wrath, brother? You know that He is a God of WRAAAAAAAAAATH!" God's wrath is synonymous with His love. In fact, His wrath is a revelation of His love toward us.

> "God's wrath is a revelation of His love toward us."

You see, God never displays His wrath until you have proven that you refuse to be corrected. His wrath is always His last attempt to convey His warning to you. But even still He does all of that in love. So if you are a new convert, I dare not confuse you. Keep following hard after God. But don't let anyone convince you that you might lose you salvation. Your salvation is not worn on your wrist like a watch. It's not worn around your neck like a necklace. It's not worn around your waist like a belt. It's not worn on your feet like shoes. It's not worn upon your head like a cap. All of those things can be easily removed. Salvation is imprinted on your soul and cannot be removed. Jesus' blood stained you in such a way that you will never be able to remove its mark. You are marked for life. Know that, and live with that revelation!

For this reason I also suffer these things; nevertheless I am not ashamed, for I know whom I have believed and am persuaded that He is able to keep what I have committed to Him until that Day (2 Timothy 1:12).

Chapter Nine

THE BIRTHRIGHT OF
THE BELIEVER

⬅〰⬅

*B*irthright is "a right, privilege, or material posses-sion to which a person is entitled by birth. An estate or civil liberty guaranteed under a constitution. During patriarchal times these privileges were primari-ly conferred upon the firstborn male child, who would become solely responsible for properly allocating each portion of the inheritance to his other siblings."

One of the things that I have not been able to under-stand, that I trust would one day change, is how most believers don't know that they have been given birthrights from the Lord Jesus Christ. In general, most people vaguely understand the concept of being born again, which is my main reason and conviction for writ-ing this book, to offer more clarity in a modern language format. Yet how is it that believers can actually be born again and not realize that they have been entitled to God-given privileges—privileges that once exercised will drastically change the quality of their lives for the better?

"Most believers don't know that they have been given birthrights from the Lord Jesus Christ."

The devil knows all about your birthrights. In fact, he is very busy trying to keep you in darkness by getting you to ignore your rights, which is a potent formula for ignorance. In life there may be many things that you choose to ignore. You may ignore complaining children or a disgruntled boss. You may ignore a nagging wife or an insensitive husband. But you should never ignore your God-given rights, those that you were spiritually born with.

The enemy wants to redirect your focus in life to things that either do not matter or that matter very little. His job is to get you to ignore the right things and get you completely focused on the cares of this life. He well knows that once you become totally focused on the cares of this life, these "weeds" will eventually choke any fruitfulness out of your life, rendering you useless to God.

Now these are the ones sown among thorns; they are the ones who hear the word, and the cares of this world, the deceitfulness of riches, and the desires for other things entering in choke the word, and it becomes unfruitful (Mark 4:18-19).

The Birthright of the Believer

What a deadly strategy! Satan gets you all focused on the wrong things so you will forfeit the right things in life, the things that lead to an abundant life. That is probably why we hear more messages about wealth and material things than we hear about the birthrights that Jesus' death ensures us. This doesn't make sense when you really think about it. Why should I chase after things when they are already mine? They already belong to me. Let me give you an illustration to clarify my point.

What if I discovered that more than fifty years ago my great-grandmother had included me in her will before she passed on into her eternal rest. Suppose that in her will she bequeathed me her entire estate. Her estate included five mansions with an estimated value of more than twenty million dollars. Added to that she left me a healthy sum of money in the form of stocks held in oil and petroleum commodities. Suppose there were classic vehicles in mint condition, a jewelry collection that featured one of the rarest diamonds of any known, and twenty million dollars of uncashed U.S. saving bonds. Could you imagine that all of this wealth actually belonged to me? This is a picture of your inheritance in Christ Jesus.

Now suppose that having said all that, I tell you that there are people who know this wealth is my inheritance and they don't want me to have it. In fact, they are doing everything in their power to steal it. Worse than their vicious attempts to steal my birthright is the fact that I have yet to realize that all of these valuable commodities and possessions actually belong to me. Suppose that I had grown up in the projects, received a second-rate education, lived in meager surroundings, and never saw the world any further than my neighborhood? This is a picture of your ignorance about your inheritance in Christ Jesus.

Isn't this pitiful? Come on, now! Wouldn't you wonder how I could be worth so much and have no idea? I didn't have to earn it any of it. It was simply left to me. How ridiculous it would be for me to go through life working like a dog to store up an inheritance for my family when someone has already done that for me. My work and labor would be in vain. More than that, I would never accomplish my goals of being able to leave an inheritance to my children. This sounds sad, but this is exactly the situation many believers are in!

Most believers have no idea that they can live life the way God intended for them to live—abundantly! Jesus said, "*The thief does not come except to steal, and to kill, and to destroy. I have come that they may have life, and that they may have it more abundantly*" (John 10:10).

When a sinner is born again, his or her old life is literally left behind. That means that whatever was tolerated or accepted as normal before will no longer have to be accepted in a new life with God. Sickness, disease, poverty and lack, and unrighteousness are all unacceptable after you have been born again. You simply cannot allow any of these things to be a common thing in your life anymore since you have an inheritance from the Father.

Just think about it, given the scenario about my great-grandmother who left me her wealthy estate. Why should I ever have to live like an impoverished person when all of that wealth is so readily available? The only thing that separates me from actually having the inheritance money is my lack of knowledge of what was actually left to me. For the believer, that should never be an issue. You should know up front that God's Son, Jesus Christ, provided for your benefit every single thing that the Father promised in His covenant to you.

> *"There should never be a moment of lack or defeat in your life after you become a believer."*

There should never be a moment of lack or defeat in your life after you become a believer. You may think, "That's too good to be true. Just because you get saved doesn't mean that you will never have problems. It doesn't mean that you will not be attacked by the enemy either." You are absolutely correct. After you receive Christ, you are not going to be attack-proof. In fact, you are going to attract attacks. But the good news is that you are not going to be defeated. You may have an attack against your finances, but the enemy cannot bankrupt you because you belong to God. In fact, your inheritance is so large that he could never bankrupt you no matter how hard he tried. You may have an attack against your health, but the devil can't kill your spirit. In fact, even in death you still win. Your spirit gets to join the Father in heaven.

"No weapon formed against you shall prosper, and every tongue which rises against you in

judgment you shall condemn. This is the heritage of the servants of the LORD, and their righteousness is from Me," says the LORD (Isaiah 54:17).

It Usually Belonged to the Firstborn

If a man has two wives, one loved and the other unloved, and they have borne him children, both the loved and the unloved, and if the firstborn son is of her who is unloved, then it shall be, on the day he bequeaths his possessions to his sons, that he must not bestow firstborn status on the son of the loved wife in preference to the son of the unloved, the true firstborn. But he shall acknowledge the son of the unloved wife as the firstborn by giving him a double portion of all that he has, for he is the beginning of his strength; the right of the firstborn is his (Deuteronomy 21:15-17).

The birthright usually belonged to the firstborn male child. Why is that important? This is essential to know because we, the body of Christ, typify His children. However, the nation of Israel represented His chosen people. They had first place in line to receive the inheritance of the Kingdom of God. However, they did not recognize Jesus as the Messiah, who was the One through whom this inheritance would come. Because they didn't receive Him, Israel forfeited her right as firstborn. That right was conferred upon those who receive Jesus as Lord and Savior. Now everyone who receives Jesus, whether Jew or Gentile, receives the inheritance from the Father.

Being firstborn or even society's favorite does not always signify God's choosing. God has sometimes chosen to give a special blessing to the underdog. Rachel and Leah, two sisters, were both married to the same man, Jacob. Rachel, the younger, was Jacob's first choice, the loved wife. Leah, the older, ended up in second place, the unloved wife. Rachel was a beautiful woman who was favored over her sister and also over other women in their cultural circle. Leah was not very attractive, nor was she popular. No one really wanted to be seen with Leah. She was definitely second rated.

The great thing is that God looks at the underdog and often gives him or her advantages to overcome their disadvantages. For many years, Rachel was barren. She couldn't give Jacob children. But Leah was able to bear children. Though Rachel was Jacob's first choice, Leah, his second choice, would become the one through whom the bloodline of the Christ child would run. What an honor!

That describes our inheritance in Christ also. We begin as underdogs, among the unfavored. We may have done things in life that were less than honorable. We may have been involved in things that did not honor God. After we repented, turned from our wicked ways, and began to follow Jesus, our old status was washed away and all things became new. The birthright usually belonged to the firstborn, but thank God that Christ made it available to all.

It's Not For Sale

Now Jacob cooked a stew; and Esau came in from the field, and he was weary. And Esau said to Jacob, "Please feed me with that same red stew, for I am weary." Therefore his name was called Edom. But Jacob said, "Sell me your birthright as of this day." And Esau said, "Look, I am about to die; so what is this birthright to me?" Then Jacob said, "Swear to me as of this day." So he swore to him, and sold his birthright to Jacob. And Jacob gave Esau bread and stew of lentils; then he ate and drank, arose, and went his way. Thus Esau despised his birthright (Genesis 25:29-34).

In life there will be times of compromise and times when compromise is totally unacceptable. In the area of your birthrights, compromise should always be totally unacceptable. You should never trade something of inferior value for something that is priceless. This is exactly what Esau did. Esau, having come in from a hard day's work, was hungry, so hungry that he diminished the value of his spiritual and most invaluable birthright. Too often, believers do the same thing. We do this by remaining in poverty, remaining in sickness, remaining in bondage when God the Father has given us an inheritance of freedom from those things. He gives us power and authority to get free and to claim the riches of His Kingdom, such as health, prosperity, and freedom from bondage. That is one of the reasons why I believe that Christians need to live a lifestyle of fasting. This is one way to receive breakthroughs into our inheritance.

Esau's appetite caused him to lose everything. He preferred to satisfy his carnal nature above his spirit man. When is the last time you put a check on your carnal nature? Is your appetite for carnal things so uncontrollable that you would actually lose the most precious gift of God? I certainly hope not. There are some things that have incomparable value in life.

> "A lifestyle of fasting is one way to receive breakthroughs into our inheritance."

Those things cannot be traded, bartered against, or sold. Your salvation is one of those things.

When you are born again, you simultaneously received inheritance papers. Everything that the King has, you have access to. Why would anyone give up all of that in exchange for a pot of stew? It seems quite foolish, doesn't it? But people do it all of the time. You have to beware and live your life with great caution knowing that the enemy desires to take everything away from you that God has given you. Let the devil know from this moment on that you don't take cheap trade-offs. Let him know that your salvation is not for sale and that your birthright is precious to you. There is absolutely nothing he could ever offer that would equate to what Christ died to give you. And that is an area of no compromise.

Here are a few scriptures concerning your inheritance.

The Spirit Himself bears witness with our spirit that we are children of God, and if children, then heirs—heirs of God and joint heirs with Christ, if indeed we suffer with Him, that we may also be glorified together (Romans 8:16-17).

In Him also we have obtained an inheritance, being predestined according to the purpose of Him who works all things according to the counsel of His will, that we who first trusted in Christ should be to the praise of His glory. In Him you also trusted, after you heard the word of truth, the gospel of your salvation; in whom also, having believed, you were sealed with the Holy Spirit of promise, who is the guarantee of our inheritance until the redemption of the purchased possession, to the praise of His glory (Ephesians 1:11-14).

Here are a couple of examples from Scripture of God's favor falling upon a younger son, or the underdog.

And Esau said, "Is he not rightly named Jacob? For he has supplanted me these two times. He took away my birthright, and now look, he has taken away my blessing!" And he said, "Have you not reserved a blessing for me?" (Genesis 27:36)

And he blessed Joseph, and said: "God, before whom my fathers Abraham and Isaac walked, the God who has fed me all my life long to this day, the Angel who has redeemed me from all evil, bless the lads; let my name be named upon them, and the name of my fathers Abraham and Isaac; and let them grow into a multitude in the midst of the earth." Now when Joseph saw that his father laid his right hand on the head of Ephraim, it displeased him; so he took hold of his father's hand to remove it from Ephraim's head to Manasseh's head. And Joseph said to his father, "Not so, my father, for this one is the firstborn; put your right hand on his head." But his father refused and said, "I know, my son, I know. He also shall become a people, and he also shall be great; but truly his younger brother shall be greater than he, and his descendants shall become a multitude of nations." So he blessed them that day, saying, "By you Israel will bless, saying, 'May God make you as Ephraim and as Manasseh!' " And thus he set Ephraim before Manasseh (Genesis 48:15-20).

Knowing Your Rights as a Believer

If you are a U.S. citizen, it benefits you to know the Constitution of the United States of America. Whatever state you reside in, it benefits you as well to know the constitution for that state. The reason is that you need to know what your rights are. Only within the framework of knowing your rights will you be able to exercise them. You can never really have true freedom until you have first understood your rights.

It is no different in the spiritual realm. We have a constitution called the Holy Bible. In it is a detailed listing of our God-given, inalienable rights. These rights are of a higher standard and authority than even the Constitution of the United States. The problem is that there are so few people who actually take the time to understand their spiritual freedoms by simply reading God's Word.

"You can never really have true freedom until you have first understood your rights."

There is a danger in not knowing your rights. When you don't know your rights, it's inevitable that you will be taken advantage of over and over again. When people are arrested for committing a crime, the first thing that the arresting officer tells them is, "You have the right to remain silent. Anything that you say, can and will be used against you in a court of law." Why do you think they bother saying that speech during every arrest? It's because they are obligated to inform you of your rights. There have been various cases where the criminal in question successfully proved that the arresting officer did not inform them of their rights. According to the law, that criminal could be acquitted of a crime he actually committed based on the negligence of the arresting officer to tell that person his rights. Why is it so crucial for the officer to do this? It's imperative because the accused criminal can't exercise his rights if he doesn't know what they are. Our rights as citizens of this country are highly valued in this society. So also are the rights that God bequeathed to His children highly valued in the Kingdom. The rights God gives us are so precious because it took the blood of His Son to earn them for us. The power of Jesus' blood is so strong that our rights as citizens of the God's Kingdom are absolutely irrevocable. No one can take them from us.

No doubt you are now asking how you can find out what all of your God-given rights are. To find out, read the Word of God. The Word of God is your official document, listing all of your rights, promises, benefits, and inheritance. What you don't know can drastically alter the quality of your life. Get to know your rights, begin acting on those rights, and watch how marvelous your life will change for the better. Be armed with the Word!

Chapter Ten

QUESTIONS AND ANSWERS

If I were teaching a seminar on the subject of under-standing the new birth, it would be customary for me to close my sessions by giving the attendees an opportunity to ask questions. You've come to the end of this reading, and you may have some very pressing questions to ask me concerning the new birth. So what I have done for your convenience is to list twenty-five of the most commonly asked questions from new converts and supply answers to those questions for you.

Perhaps the questions that are listed are not exactly what you had in mind, or perhaps they are. Whatever the case might be, I am certain that many of the answers provided will be a starting point for you to build on. However, if your questions are totally different from the ones that are listed, I will be very glad to answer your questions. Simply write to me at my ministry address, which is listed in the front of this book. It will be my privilege to respond to your inquiry as you continue to grow stronger in the things of God.

Question 1: When I received Jesus into my life I did not really feel any emotional kinds of feelings. My friend told me that if I really received Jesus, then I would know it by the feeling that I had. Is it necessary for me to have a particular feeling or emotion to be saved?

Answer: No, that is not true. You do not have to feel anything at all in order to validate that you have been born again. Remember that salvation is by God's grace, but it is appropriated to you through faith, not feelings and emotions. Your emotions change like the wind. Some days you are happy; other days you are sad. At times you feel wealthy and often you may feel pretty broke. If feelings were the basis for your salvation, you would be saved one day and lost the next. What if Jesus returned for His church on the day you were not feeling saved? Would you be left behind? Of course not! Thank God salvation does not work that way.

Perhaps your friend felt an emotional feeling because that is how God chose to manifest Himself to her. He does not manifest Himself to everybody the same way. An emotional feeling can be a by-product of salvation for some people; however, the feeling itself is not salvation. You are saved because God's Word declares it. That is the only thing you need to base your salvation on.

That if you confess with your mouth the Lord Jesus and believe in your heart that God has raised Him from the dead, you will be saved. For with the heart one believes unto righteousness, and with the mouth confession is made unto salvation (Romans 10:9-10).

Question 2: Do I have to confess *all* of my sins in order to be saved?

Answer: No. If you literally had to confess every sin that you've ever committed since you were born, it would probably take a few weeks to list them all, and that's if you work non-stop around the clock. Added to that, you probably would not be able to reconstruct a list of all of your sins because you wouldn't be able to remember them. Some people falsely believe that you have to tell it all. Maybe man requires that of people, but God does not.

The Bible tells us that God casts all of our sins deep into the depths of a sea. Once put there, they will never be remembered again. This means that He takes all of our sins and removes them far from us to where they will never be recovered.

God is not as concerned about your listing and identifying sins as He is with getting you to understand the power of His forgiveness. He wants you to realize that His forgiveness comes to anyone that simply asks for it. God is in the forgiveness business. When you ask God to forgive your "sin" (singular) all of your "sins" (plural) are forgiven without having to give Him a detailed list.

*He will again have compassion on us, and will
subdue our iniquities. You will cast all our sins
into the depths of the sea* (Micah 7:19).

Question 3: How long do I have to be saved before I am
no longer considered a babe in Christ?

Answer: In my forty-plus years of ministry, I have
actually seen people who have been saved for five,
ten, fifteen, and even twenty years that still act as if
they are babies in Christ. In fact, they even act like
they are simply babies in a literal sense. On the other
hand, I have seen brothers and sisters right in my
local church who have received salvation and within
a few short months have become strong disciples.

Spiritual maturity is not a matter of age or
time—it is a matter of determination and ambition.
How badly do you want it? If you want all that God
has to offer and you have a determination to receive
it, time won't be a factor. You will be inclined to
spend many hours in the Word, studying and learning God's Law. When you do this, God will advance
you beyond your years and mature you in His ways.
If you want to grow up, do the things that spiritual
grown-ups do, like read the Word every day, regularly attend services, practice praying and fasting,
faithfully tithe and give offerings, and seek God with
all of your heart.

A word of caution—do not try to grow up too
fast. The Christian life has some pertinent lessons
that every believer needs to learn that cannot be

learned in an instant. Some lessons take time. Take pleasure in your baby stages in the Lord and enjoy them while they last. In time you will grow, and as you do, you will be given greater spiritual responsibilities. Even though God does expect all of us to grow and develop into a mature being, in the final analysis, we are all still God's children.

Study to shew thyself approved unto God, a workman that needeth not to be ashamed, rightly dividing the word of truth (2 Timothy 2:15 KJV).

Question 4: I grew up in the Catholic church and all of my life I confessed my sins to the priest. Now that I am born again, to whom do I confess my sins now?

Answer: The Bible makes it clear that there is no one who can forgive sins other than Jesus. That precludes all men. The priest neither has the right nor the authority to forgive anyone's sins. When a person has confessed his sins to the priest, that person is still as sinful after his confession as he was before his confession. The Bible tells us to confess our sins to Jesus. He is our mediator, which means that He goes to the Father on our behalf when we fail God. When He does that, He reminds the Father of the price that He paid on the cross for your sins. The Father then has to forgive your sins because Jesus has already paid your price. Think of it as being like a gift that was purchased by a friend or loved one. You don't have to give them money in exchange for the gift they purchased for you. It's already paid for. Since Jesus Christ is the One who paid the high price for your sin, He is the One who has the power to forgive you of that sin.

For there is one God and one Mediator between God and men, the Man Christ Jesus, who gave Himself a ransom for all, to be testified in due time (1 Timothy 2:5-6).

Question 5: If I commit a sin after I received salvation, do I have to get saved over again?

Answer: Once you have asked God to forgive your sins, you don't need to be paranoid about every single sin that you may commit. Now, I am in no way suggesting that you live your life recklessly, not regarding God's Word, and looking for opportunities to sin. But if you sinned by commission or omission, you can be justified or made righteous by the grace of God. Don't be mistaken—your sins are not justified, but *you* are through Christ's work on the cross. Because of that, you don't need to keep on getting saved over and over again.

Over the years, I've seen people, who did not quite understand God's power to forgive, respond week after week to the invitation to be saved. They did not realize that all they needed to do was to ask God to forgive them, receive His forgiveness, and just move on. When you continue to get saved over and over, that makes it appear as if your original salvation experience was not authentic. The real meaning of salvation continually points us to Jesus, who is always willing to receive us with open arms when we have fallen or gone astray. If you've sinned after salvation, ask for forgiveness, not to be saved again. True salvation happens one time.

> *But now the righteousness of God apart from the law is revealed, being witnessed by the Law and the Prophets, even the righteous-ness of God, through faith in Jesus Christ, to all and on all who believe. For there is no dif-ference; for all have sinned and fall short of the glory of God, being justified freely by His grace through the redemption that is in Christ Jesus* (Romans 3:21-24).

Question 6: Can I get saved anywhere or do I have to be in a church building to be genuinely saved?

Answer: You can get saved anywhere. I have heard of people getting saved in their own homes, in automo-biles, at weddings, and even at funeral services. I know of some people who have even gotten saved right outside of a nightclub. You don't have to be in a sanctuary with stained glass windows and all of the other trappings of traditional churches. People have said, "Pastor, I want to get saved, but I want to do it with my whole family at church next month." Although that sounds really nice and family oriented, it's not God's desire for you to continue to put off the most important decision that you could possibly make. Tomorrow really isn't promised to you. So you should live today as if it were your very last one, making all of the preparations necessary to be with Jesus. The place is not important but the time is.

> *And if it seems evil to you to serve the LORD, choose for yourselves this day whom you will serve, whether the gods which your fathers served that were on the other side of the River, or the gods of the Amorites, in whose land you dwell. But as for me and my house, we will serve the LORD* (Joshua 24:15).

Question 7: If I just live a good life and treat everyone fairly, why do I need to be saved?

Answer: Whether or not you live a good life and treat everyone with respect does not have any bearing on whether you will inherit eternal life. Salvation does not come to anyone because he or she worked for it. You cannot merit or earn salvation because it is not for sale. If it were, the rich would have eternal life and the poor would die. Salvation is free, but it is provided through God's grace.

Living a morally conscientious life and treating others well will definitely ensure that we have a quality life in this earth. However, if you desire to have a quality life for eternity to come, you have to realize that you cannot work for it. You have to realize and accept that Jesus is the only way for you to be saved from this wicked and perverse generation.

> *For by grace you have been saved through faith, and that not of yourselves; it is the gift*

of God, not of works, lest anyone should boast. For we are His workmanship, created in Christ Jesus for good works, which God prepared beforehand that we should walk in them (Ephesians 2:8-10).

Question 8: I have friends who are great people, but they belong to various religions that are not Christian. If they die, will they perish simply because they did not accept the name of Jesus?

Answer: There is no other name in heaven or on earth by which men and women can receive salvation other than through the name of Jesus—no exceptions. In these particular days, we have experienced an enormous amount of compromise concerning this issue. In America, we try to be so accepting of everybody else's religious faith and of their gods that we have become totally confused as to who the real One and only true God is. The body of Christ makes no mistake about who God is—His name is Jesus.

Your friends may be very wonderful people. They may have very wonderful dispositions, and that is good. However, if they do not accept the name of Jesus, they will not enter the Kingdom of God. That is not my determination; it is God's Word.

This is the "stone which was rejected by you builders, which has become the chief cornerstone." Nor is there salvation in any other, for there is no other name under heaven given

among men by which we must be saved
(Acts 4:11-12).

Question 9: Once I am saved, is it necessary for me to become a member of the local church?

Answer: It is very necessary for you to become a member of a Bible-believing church. The only way that your faith is going to develop is through hearing God's Word as regularly as possible. If you don't hear God's Word consistently, you will not be able to grow.

Also, you need the local church for accountability reasons. There are far too many "loose cannons" in the body of Christ who are not accountable to anyone, not even to God. They'll hide behind the guise of religiosity, claiming that they can serve God without going to church, but that is simply untrue. If we are going to truly serve God, then we have to do it His way. And His way requires us to assemble together to worship with people of like precious faith.

People within the local church will be able to help you to identify the areas in which you may need strengthening. If you don't attend church regularly you will not be able to be strengthened, since nobody will really know anything about you. Stop hiding. Come out of your closet of fear and become a faithful and integral part of the local church. It will be one of the best decisions that you ever made.

And let us consider one another in order to stir up love and good works, not forsaking the assembling of ourselves together, as is the manner of some, but exhorting one another, and so much the more as you see the Day approaching (Hebrews 10:24-25).

Question 10: If I get saved, do I have to give all of my money to the church?

Answer: One of the most foolish statements that I have heard is, "I ain't giving all my money to the church," or "If you join that church, you are going to have to give them all of your money." In nearly fifty years of ministry, I have never once witnessed anybody that gave *all* of his or her money to the church. The only people I know who ever did such a thing are the early believers mentioned in the book of Acts chapter 4. They sold all of their possessions and gave the money to the apostles. Other than that occurrence, I don't know of any contemporary examples.

You will, however, give *some* money to the church. God requires His people to give a tenth of what they earn and additional offerings to finance the work of the Kingdom. Simple commonsense will tell you that a tenth has never equaled one hundred percent or all of anything. Most of the time, people who are not accustomed to attending and supporting the local church will tend to make such frivolous remarks because they really don't know any better and they do not have correct information. When God truly saves you, money will never be an issue. He becomes the provider of all your needs. You should want to give your tithes and offerings to be obedient to God's Word. When He is your provider, you won't have a reason to make a big deal about it. You will want to do anything that pleases God.

> *"Bring all the tithes into the storehouse, that there may be food in My house, and try Me now in this," says the LORD of hosts, "if I will not open for you the windows of heaven and pour out for you such blessing that there will not be room enough to receive it. And I will rebuke the devourer for your sakes, so that he will not destroy the fruit of your ground, nor shall the vine fail to bear fruit for you in the field," says the LORD of hosts; "and all nations will call you blessed, for you will be a delightful land," says the LORD of hosts* (Malachi 3:10-12).

Question 11: I got saved but I have a man living with me that is not my husband. Should I ask him to leave, or do I have to leave?

> Answer: In any given situation we always desire God's best. And God's best is always in concert with His Word. His Word does not uphold and condone cohabitation. In fact, cohabitation is an affront to God and to His original purpose for the family. When God saves you, He does not want to continually revisit your sins, particularly since they are forgiven. However, He does want you to realize that since your sins are forgiven you have a moral

responsibility to refrain from those sins from that point on. It does not really matter which one leaves. That will be decided through logical reasoning. The point is that one of you will need to leave so that God's blessings can flow freely and uninterrupted in your newly saved life.

> *Now the works of the flesh are evident, which are: adultery, fornication, uncleanness, lewdness, idolatry, sorcery, hatred, contentions, jealousies, outbursts of wrath, selfish ambitions, dissensions, heresies, envy, murders, drunkenness, revelries, and the like; of which I tell you beforehand, just as I also told you in time past, that those who practice such things will not inherit the kingdom of God* (Galatians 5:19-21).

Question 12: Do I have to change my style of dress after I get saved, or can I continue to wear what I choose to wear?

Answer: God is far more concerned about your heart than He is about your clothes. There are some people who dress as though they are "the holy and pious," yet they live like they are the greatest of sinners. Their style dressing does not reflect who they really are. I believe that the Holy Spirit has the ability to teach you how you should dress after you have received Christ. Fashions will continue to change as long as we are alive. You should neither chase fashions, always trying to keep up with the latest fads, nor should fashions chase you. You don't have to dress in clothes that are totally outdated and irrelevant to today's culture. Sometimes, your apparel can actually be used as a tool to win people to the Lord.

I have always loved to look and dress my absolute best. That's something that has been in me since I was a child. Over the years, I've used my image as an effective tool to attract people to Jesus. Your image should always be a mirror of Christ's image to the people around you. So if something is lewd or sensual, you should probably refrain from wearing such a thing. However, if something is fashionable and relevant, you do not have to shy away from it, thinking it's worldly. God uses all kinds of things as tools to win the world. Clothing is just one of those many things. You can use your clothing to bring glory either to God or to yourself. The choice is yours.

> *I beseech you therefore, brethren, by the mercies of God, that you present your bodies a living sacrifice, holy, acceptable to God, which is your reasonable service. And do not be conformed to this world, but be transformed by the renewing of your mind, that you may prove what is that good and acceptable and perfect will of God* (Romans 12:1-2).

Question 13: How about makeup and jewelry? Someone at my workplace goes to a church that condemns women who wear makeup, and they also have prohibitions against wearing jewelry. She told me if I wear these things that I will go to hell. Is that true?

Answer: There are some churches that teach a legalistic gospel. They believe that if you keep all their rules and regulations that God will approve you. The truth of the matter is that you really can't do anything within your own power and in your flesh to earn God's approval rating on your life. He already loves you just the way you are. In fact, the Bible says while you were still in sin Christ died for you. So anyone who teaches that wearing jewelry or makeup will bring you eternal damnation is misinformed.

It may very well be that your coworker is a well-intentioned person with a genuine heart toward God. However, she has been given wrong information that has been passed down from one generation to the next. Such teachings were not measured against God's Word. Over time, any man-made doctrine may become accepted if it lasts long enough, whether it's true or not. Wrong information can introduce prejudicial practices. In our American society, we have witnessed prejudicial behaviors toward women, blacks, Jews, and people of varying faiths. Just because people behave a certain way does not make it correct or righteous.

In the same manner, just because people have accepted a particular doctrine does not mean that it is from the Lord. What you wear does not save you. It has nothing to do with your eternal life. If wearing gold were a sin, then why would God pave the streets of glory in gold? Don't feel condemned by people who choose to stay in bondage to such prejudices. The Lord has set you free and that is all that should matter to you.

For the LORD takes pleasure in His people; He will beautify the humble with salvation (Psalm 149:4).

Question 14: If I die before I get water baptized, will I go to hell?

Answer: Our God is a God of mercy. And we have to begin and end with that in mind. I thoroughly believe in water baptism by immersion. The Bible clearly articulates that every believer should be baptized. Baptism is a public confession of our identification with Jesus. To refuse to be baptized is to refute the name of Jesus. This would be in complete opposition to having accepted Him as your Lord. Any person who claims to love the Lord should want to be baptized. On this question, I believe the Lord looks at the intent of our hearts. If it's your full intention to be baptized, and it should be, but something happens to prevent it and you die, you will not lose your salvation because of it. There are circumstances that may prevent a person from being baptized before his or her death. We see one example of this in the book of Luke, chapter 23. One of the thieves dying on the cross next to Jesus affirms Jesus as the awaited Messiah. Obviously this man had no opportunity before him to be baptized.

He was dying, yet Jesus tells him, *"Assuredly, I say to you, today you will be with Me in Paradise"* (Luke 23:43). Jesus grants the thief entrance into heaven. So there are times when baptism is not possible; however, God's Word stresses very strongly a believer's obligation to be baptized. You should never treat your need to be baptized lightly. Other than being physically prevented from being baptized, there really is no other excuse for not obeying God's Word on this. If you are born again and have not been baptized immediately, talk with your pastor about getting baptized. It is always better to be on the safe side with Jesus.

> *He who believes and is baptized will be saved; but he who does not believe will be condemned* (Mark 16:16).

Question 15: What does it mean to be sanctified?

Answer: *To be sanctified* literally means "to be different from or to be set apart." *Sanctification* and *holiness* are words that can be used interchangeably. In the old-time holiness church, the church that I grew up in, holiness was measured an entirely different way from how God measures holiness. Our version of holiness was measured solely by what clothes a person wore, by what places a person went to or didn't go to, and with which people a person would affiliate himself. Our old-time holiness was not God's version of holiness.

Simply put, *holiness* is "the character and nature of God." God does not merely act holy—He is holy. It is a distinct part of His composition. So if I say that you are sanctified it simply means that you reflect the character and nature of God. You are different from worldly people. Being sanctified also means that you have a different worldview from the rest of society. You have adopted God's worldview. And believe me, when you choose to side with God, you will be considered very peculiar and strange. The world will set you apart without your asking them to. Don't wait for others to set you apart— sanctify yourself. Be proud that you identify with a holy God. If that distinction makes you different, and you are labeled odd because of that, wear your "sanctification" proudly as a badge of honor.

> *Then God blessed the seventh day and sanctified it, because in it He rested from all His work which God had created and made* (Genesis 2:3).

> *Get up, sanctify the people, and say, "Sanctify yourselves for tomorrow, because thus says the LORD God of Israel: 'There is an accursed thing in your midst, O Israel; you cannot stand before your enemies until you take away the accursed thing from among you'"* (Joshua 7:13).

Question 16: I've heard people tell me that once I am saved I need to ask God to fill me with the Holy Spirit

158

and that I should speak in tongues. Is this true, and if it is, will you please explain its relevance?

Answer: Every believer needs to be baptized in the Holy Spirit. After a person has received salvation, he or she should immediately begin to seek the Christ, who is the baptizer in the Holy Spirit. The gift of tongues is not the only nor initial evidence of being baptized in the Holy Ghost, although it can be. Love is the most constant and enduring quality within a person who has genuinely been baptized in the Holy Spirit. Baptism in the Holy Spirit is a baptism of God. And, God is love. Therefore, you can speak in tongues all day long, but if your life is not seasoned with the love of God, all of your tongue talking is in vain.

Coupled with the love of God, speaking in tongues is a dynamic force that accomplishes great things in the spirit and earth realms. I believe that you should pray in tongues, just as the Word of God says, to build up your most holy faith and to edify the body.

When the Day of Pentecost had fully come, they were all with one accord in one place. And suddenly there came a sound from heaven, as of a rushing mighty wind, and it filled the whole house where they were sitting. Then there appeared to them divided tongues, as of fire, and one sat upon each of them. And they were all filled with the Holy Spirit and began to speak with other tongues, as the Spirit gave them utterance (Acts 2:1-4).

Question 17: I'm saved now, and I really want to stay focused. What are some practical things that I can do on a regular basis to keep me moving in the righteous direction?

Answer: There is nothing that a new believer can do that will benefit him or her more than staying in the Word on a regular basis. Early on you have to make a habit and routine of listening to the Word of God. The faith that you need will only come after you have heard and heard and heard again. Often you may have to listen to the same word over and over until it becomes second nature for you. There is a phrase, "practice makes perfect."

Just like a person who wants to develop a very muscular body has to work out regularly at the gym in order to stay in shape, the believer also has to practice reading and applying God's Word. Notice that I said both reading *and* applying the Word. It does little good to read your Bible if you don't apply what you read to your everyday life. If you want to be focused on the things of God, you are going to have to remain in the practicing mode, always striving for perfection in Christ.

So then faith comes by hearing, and hearing by the word of God (Romans 10:17).

Question 18: I've heard my minister say that giving money will ensure my blessings on earth. How is this possible? And, can I be blessed if I choose not to give any money at all?

Answer: Giving always secures blessing for you. You cannot be blessed in a biblical sense if you have money to give and choose not to give it. All throughout the Bible, God tries to get the much-needed message across to His people that giving determines our living. Many people try to follow man-made systems that promise blessing, yet always fall short. God is the One who empowers people to get wealth. And when He does that, He doesn't do it so that greed and avarice will consume our flesh. He financially prospers His people so that His Kingdom will be established in the earth.

The main thing to recognize is that God only gives financial increase to those He is sure can handle it. So, how can you determine whether or not you can handle financial increase? It's simple really. If you refuse to tithe and give offerings out of what you have received, then you don't qualify. If you honor God with your tithes and the offering, then God will inevitably give you more.

Then you say in your heart, "My power and the might of my hand have gained me this wealth." And you shall remember the LORD your God, for it is He who gives you power to get wealth, that He may establish His covenant which He swore to your fathers, as it is this day (Deuteronomy 8:17-18).

Question 19: I heard someone say during communion that if you eat and drink "unworthily" you may damn yourself. I've also heard people say that if you take communion when you have sin in your life you automatically disqualify yourself. Is this true?

Answer: The Lord's Supper represents the body of our Lord and Savior Jesus Christ. There are varying ways to look at this question. Some people truly believe that if you have any sin in your life, then you disqualify yourself from taking communion. If this were true, most people in the body of Christ would never take communion. We all do things that do not meet the mark of God, at times without our even knowing it. I believe that we become unworthy in the biblical sense when we do not honor the body of the Lord. This can mean living a lifestyle of unrepentant sinfulness. If a person continues to willfully sin, then in a way he invalidates the sacrament of Holy Communion. So we need to be living a lifestyle of righteousness before God.

Just as important is that we cannot afford to disregard other parts of Christ's body. I fully realize that my brothers and sisters in the body of Christ may not all think like me or do things the way that we do them at our church. Nonetheless, they are still my brothers and sisters in the Lord. I have Lutheran, Baptist, Methodist, Pentecostal, Anglican, and non-denominational brothers and sisters all over the world. To discount them and to discount their connection to the body of Christ because they don't do things like I do is tantamount to dishonoring Christ's body, hence making me disqualified to receive communion. I then become unworthy.

> *Therefore whoever eats this bread or drinks this cup of the Lord in an unworthy manner will be guilty of the body and blood of the Lord. But let a man examine himself, and so let him eat of the bread and drink of the cup. For he who eats and drinks in an unworthy manner eats and drinks judgment to himself, not discerning the Lord's body. For this reason many are weak and sick among you, and many sleep. For if we would judge ourselves, we would not be judged* (1 Corinthians 11:27-31).

Question 20: I'm saved, but my spouse is not saved and refutes everything that I believe. What should I do?

Answer: Never argue with a person who does not really understand why he or she is arguing in the first place. If your spouse is not saved, he or she is only going to get saved through your daily example before them. Unfortunately, family members can at times be the most difficult people to minister to. Because they are family, they are so familiar with you that they do not respect your anointing. I believe that you should continue to pray for your spouse. Ask God to send someone into your spouse's life that he will be receptive to where salvation is concerned. Maybe your loved one won't get saved through your witness, but will through someone else's. The most important thing is that he gets saved. God answers the prayers of His people. If you are unwilling to give up on your spouse, then God won't quit either.

> For the unbelieving husband is sanctified by the wife, and the unbelieving wife is sanctified by the husband; otherwise your children would be unclean, but now they are holy (1 Corinthians 7:14).

Question 21: My spouse becomes very argumentative and often abusive toward me when I go to church. Should I continue to go to church anyway, or should I just quit?

Answer: Under no circumstances should you totally quit going to church. A person who is not saved cannot make a determination on whether you go to church or not. You've got to understand that this is all about a personal relationship between you and God. An unsaved person is blind and will not be able to see spiritual things like you do. You have to stay firmly grounded in the ministry that God has planted you in. This is an area where you must put all of your trust in the Lord, not in man. Make a firm commitment to walk in love and peace with your spouse, but do not compromise your faith. And do not for one moment give the enemy the opportunity to cause confusion. Let God fight your battle. He wins all of the time.

Pursue peace with all people, and holiness, without which no one will see the Lord: looking carefully lest anyone fall short of the grace of God; lest any root of bitterness springing up cause trouble, and by this many become defiled (Hebrews 12:14-15).

Question 22: My spouse does not care for my pastor. He does not have any real reasons for his dislike. I believe it's just a personal problem. How should I respond to this?

Answer: The ultimate goal should be for you to win your spouse to the Lord. As with anyone else, winning souls always requires godly wisdom, especially when it is your family that you are trying to win. A lot of times a man especially does not like the pastor of his spouse because the pastor is a constant reminder to him that he is out of order. In a family setting, it is the husband's role to lead spiritual things. However, God is not going to wait on men for eternity to get their acts together. I've heard of men telling their wives not to go to this church or that church because they don't like the pastor. A man really does not have that kind of authority if he is not saved. He cannot choose a spiritual path for his wife if he does not know the Lord. Only when a man is truly born again can he lead his wife and family in the things of God.

Again, do not quarrel, but rather show your spouse love. More than likely his dislike of the pastor is a personal problem that he will have to get over. If you go to church somewhere else, he will know that you are easily moved and will not have any respect for you. If you stay rooted, he may be a bit upset, but he will have a profound respect and honor for you. Choose honor.

The fruit of the righteous is a tree of life, and he who wins souls is wise (Proverbs 11:30).

Question 23: I am a teenager and my friend invited me to her church where I received Christ as my personal Savior. I thought that my mom would be excited when I shared the news with her about my newfound faith in Christ. To my surprise, she was angry and opposed to my going to church. How should I deal with this?

Answer: This can be a very touchy area to deal with. The first thing to understand is that you are obligated to honor your parents and obey them. However, you are also mandated to serve God. Because you may still live at home, I would suggest that you obey your parents' rule. However, I believe that you should search out alternate ways of being able to be fed. Keep your prayer life very consistent and read your Bible. Ask God to make a provision for you to be able to serve Him without persecution from your parents. In the final analysis, you will have to choose God over them.

When my father and my mother forsake me, then the LORD will take care of me (Psalm 27:10).

Question 24: I work for a company that produces tobacco products. I realize that cigarette smoking and ingesting cigarette smoke leads to premature death. I am saved now and desire to live my life for God wholeheartedly and sincerely. Must I leave my job in order to be pleasing to God?

> Answer: When a person is born again, the spirit of God resides on the inside of her. I believe that you will have to ask God whether or not this place of employment is the right place for you. If you are feeling great conviction not to work there anymore, then you need to follow your heart's conviction. But my best advice to you is to seek God concerning the matter. His answer will be far greater and far more personal than mine.
>
> > *And I will pray the Father, and He will give you another Helper, that He may abide with you forever—the Spirit of truth, whom the world cannot receive, because it neither sees Him nor knows Him; but you know Him, for He dwells with you and will be in you* (John 14:16-17).

Question 25: After I get saved, how long will it take for me to start my own ministry?

> Answer: The first thing that a person should do after getting saved is to learn God's Word. I've seen so many people fail miserably in ministry by trying to step into it too soon. The most important thing that you can do once you get saved is to spend time with

Jesus. And not until you've done that will you be qualified to minister to anyone. Ministry requires developing spiritual leadership skills. You have to master being a follower first before you can lead. Ask your minister if he or she has anything that you can do to serve in the house of the Lord. The greatest leaders are those who embrace the Christian message of serving. If you really want to be at the top, serve your way to the top. Jesus did it; look where it got Him.

> *For as we have many members in one body, but all the members do not have the same function, so we, being many, are one body in Christ, and individually members of one another. Having then gifts differing according to the grace that is given to us, let us use them: if prophecy, let us prophesy in proportion to our faith; or ministry, let us use it in our ministering; he who teaches, in teaching; he who exhorts, in exhortation; he who gives, with liberality; he who leads, with diligence; he who shows mercy, with cheerfulness* (Romans 12:4-8).

> *And being found in appearance as a man, He humbled Himself and became obedient to the point of death, even the death of the cross. Therefore God also has highly exalted Him and given Him the name which is above every name, that at the name of Jesus every knee should bow, of those in heaven, and of those on earth, and of those under the earth,*

and that every tongue should confess that Jesus Christ is Lord, to the glory of God the Father (Philippians 2:8-11).

ABOUT THE AUTHOR

❧❧

Dr. John E. Wilson serves as an apostle to the greater body of Christ by establishing new churches in the United States and in the Caribbean. He is revered among his peers as a spiritual father to many pastors and leaders. Dr. Wilson also ministers on *Voice of Deliverance*, a television program broadcast over PAX, in addition to airing a radio program on WKND in the Hartford, Connecticut, area. He has served as co-host of the New England Prophetic Conference for many years. Dr. Wilson holds doctorate of divinity and theology degrees and has received numerous awards and citations.